To Lia,

MW00965130

2018

The Pink Rose

&

Love Was My Business: Memoirs of a Matchmaker

by

Sylvia D. London

Best Wishes + Happy Reading

Love, Sylvia

Copyright

Copyright © 2018 by Sylvia D. London. All rights reserved.
This book or any portion thereofmay not be reproduced or used
in any manner whatsoeverwithout the express written
permission of the publisher except for the use of brief quotations
in a book review.
Printed in the United States of America
First Printing, 2018

The Pink Rose

by

Sylvia D. London

Chapter One: The Meeting

Cynthia had heard his name mentioned by members of the small church. It was always mentioned respectfully and it seemed that he stood out as a leader. She had heard that he had broken off from the main group and had started his own flock of followers. It was at a church service that she had first seen him.

"Hi Hal," a voice had said and her eyes moved toward the person addressed. She had imagined him a little younger and better looking. His appearance was rugged. A thin angular face and jaw, a tall bony hunched back and shoulders. Intense eyes looked out from behind the thickly rimmed glasses as he exchanged greetings with the one who greeted him. He was an ugly man, with thin brown hair and blue eyes. She noticed he wore no tie, which she later realized was out of character for him. The group then moved to find their seats as the guest speaker was about to be introduced. Cynthia found her place with some friends and did not encounter Hal again that day or to think of him again.

Cynthia had recently moved to Vancouver to start a new life. She had made a decision and used all the principles taught by her church to achieve her goal. She had landed a job at a department store as a decorator consultant. Her position included visiting homes and selling blinds and draperies. Cynthia was an attractive woman with dark hair and eyes. Although not religious, she lived her life by spiritual principles. The Church group had become a family to her, being in a strange city beginning a new job, not knowing many people and all things being unfamiliar. Then she had learned that the minister and his wife, Bill and Bonnie, had decided to return to California. She felt pangs of sadness over this as though Mom and Dad were abandoning her. The couple had provided her with friendship and a sense of belonging, something she had missed most of her life.

For a time, she hoped that they would change their minds and stay, but when the members of the church began planning a farewell party, she finally accepted her loss. To bid a humorous and affectionate goodbye to the couple, a program of little songs and skits were presented. It was during one of these songs that she encountered Hal for the second time.

Among a group dressed as sheep singing, "We're little lost sheep but we've found our way," his intense eyes were looking out of sheep eyeholes, was Hal. She also recognized his bony, angular shoulders.

In the weeks that followed, after the couple had left, some of the more serious members invited guest speakers to fill in on Sunday mornings until a new minister could be selected. Hal was one of these. It was then that Cynthia was officially introduced to him. He wore a shirt and tie this time, which Cynthia learned was typical of him. He gave an interesting sermon but Cynthia was a bit uneasy with his evangelical style. He didn't say "Halleluiah, Praise the Lord" but almost.

It was Jesse, his new assistant, who was from the church and had gone with Hal to his new church, who actually introduced them. She told Cynthia about all the classes they were offering at Hal's center and then made a point of introducing her to Hal. Later, Cynthia discovered Jesse was actually recruiting people for Hal's centre.

Cynthia was anxious to continue her studies in Science of Mind or New Thought and since there would be none at her church she decided that she would call Hal to inquire about what he had to offer. On her next day off, she took the card provided to her by Jesse and dialed the number. When he answered the phone she said "This is Cynthia Daniels from the Surrey Church calling. I am interested in taking your third year class and would like some information."

In a deep voice, and she imagined his intense spectacled eyes, he explained to her some of the details of the course.

"What makes you think you should be taking this course?" he asked.

"Well," she stammered, "I took first and second year in Calgary with Joan Dexter."

"Why don't you come and try our centre sometime, find out what we are all about?"

A little disappointed that he was not more persuasive, she thanked him and decided that she may try his group sometime. She still had two weeks to make up her mind about taking the course.

Feeling unusually fragile, unsupported and alone that week, she stumbled outside a customer's house while wearing high-heeled shoes and carrying heavy cases. The shooting pains in her ankle started later in the day. The store nurse, looking for something constructive to do, sent her home bandaged and on worker's compensation. Cynthia then went home to lick her wounds. She lay down on the couch, something she did when she was depressed and put ice on her ankle.

In the church it was common to ask an experienced person, a practitioner to pray for you if you were in need. Since her beloved couple was gone the only person she could think of was Hal. She dialed his home number and listened to his deep voice on the answering machine saying he would return the call as soon as possible. She noted that the message appeared to be from the home of a single man not a couple as it said "I" rather than "we." At least she wasn't bothering a spouse. The next morning, he returned her call.

"Hello this is Hal Carter, I am sorry I got in so late that I wasn't able to get back to you last night." the deep voice said.

"Thank you for calling," replied Cynthia

"How can I help you?" he asked, getting right down to business.

"I've sprained my ankle. I was wondering if you would say a prayer for me."

"What would you like me to pray for?" he asked.
They always asked that question which made Cynthia feel put on the spot. Prayer always had to relate to cause and effect.

"I guess I feel unsupported" she said. "I want healing and to feel supported by God."

He said a short prayer and then asked "Are you married or

are you alone?"

"I'm separated," she replied.

"How long have you been separated?" he asked.

"About three years," she answered, and then added. "I've been married twice."

"I'm separated and have been married twice too." he volunteered, as if he were keeping score.

He concluded the conversation by saying he would have his assistant Jesse call her later. One minute he was being super personal and the next he was dismissing her. She was also left with a feeling of being a victim, that he was just a little too sympathetic. The third thing she noted was that he was single.

It was a week or ten days later, after her mother's visit and her ankle had healed, that she decided to try out Hal's center on a Thursday night and to give a donation for the prayer and support they had given her. When she arrived at the seedy old building on Broadway, after a half hour drive, she looked around the lecture room. She spotted Hal sitting near the back beside a blonde haired woman. Was this his girlfriend?

A female singer with a blues kind of voice was singing John Lennon's "Imagine" When she sang the line, "No religion too," Cynthia wondered how Hal could have a church without religion, without God.

The service began in the usual way with Jesse doing the opening prayer. Then Hal got up and gave a considerably less dramatic talk than he had that day in Surrey. The point of it seemed to be how his church had been nothing more than an idea, a Divine Idea in the Mind of God and now it had come into reality, starting with a small group who met in his apartment. Cynthia noted he said "my" rather than "our "apartment.

At the end of the service, everyone as usual, formed a circle, joined hands and sang, "Let There be Peace on Earth." She could hear the man beside her singing awfully loud, shouting out the words. As the song ended, she glanced sideways and saw that it was Hal. He had moved to her part of the circle and taken her hand. Was it on purpose? After the song ended, people stayed around to drink coffee and chat. It was obvious that Hal was going out of his way to talk to Cynthia." Have you decided to take our class?" he asked. "I put your name on a slip of paper on my tack board."

"I think so but I'm not one hundred per cent sure," Cynthia replied. She went on to tell him about the recent visit she had from her mother and how empty she felt when her mother had gone. "Why does it have to be that way?" she asked.

"I have the same problem with my parents," he said, "The truth is we can never please them. They do it so we won't ever give up trying. Disapproving of us keeps us under their control."

The coffee ended, and Cynthia drove the half hour home. The next week she began the course.

Chapter Two: The Connection

One of Cynthia's friends from the Surrey Church had decided to take the course too, so she had someone to ride with. It was a long trip from where she lived as it took over half an hour to get there and get parked.

About fifteen people had enrolled in the course and the majority of them were women. This was always the case with self-improvement. Women were the ones trying to improve. Cynthia checked out the two men in the class and found one of them sported a huge gold wedding band and the other was obviously gay.

Hal was not really prepared for the class as he seemed to be operating off the cuff, not too sure about what he was going to do next. A large aggressive woman suggested that we try to define God or at least think of words, which described the nature of God. Hal must have agreed that this was as good a place as any to begin, because that is how the first class started. It was interesting but not at all like anything Cynthia had taken before where classes were structured and pre planned.

Thus the autumn began for Cynthia-burying herself in her work and traveling to Vancouver on Wednesday nights. Faithfully she completed the assignments; not having any certainty about the direction her studies would take her. Hal seemed genuinely interested in her as a person and as time went on she couldn't help but feel she had known him before, that she had known him always, as if they were somehow connected in some spiritual way. He would always smile at her and gush over her when she arrived, giving her lots of attention.

In one class, he asked each person to make a positive affirmation about herself, or himself, and then the group would give each one individual support in knowing that the affirmations were true. Cynthia's was "I am loved, loveable and loving," to which Hal responded sympathetically. There were other indications that he regarded her as special. He started kissing her on the lips when she came to class.

One woman in the class was a member of Toastmaster. Cynthia noticed that Hal always called upon her to give her presentation last. This was the toastmaster's policy to always save the best for last. Cynthia was usually one of the first to be called upon so she realized how Hal had labeled her.

One Sunday at the Surrey Church, where services were still being held with guest speakers, Hal was once again asked to speak. This time Cynthia was called upon to do what was called the "front end". It included the welcome, announcements, an opening prayer and introduction of the guest speaker. She pre wrote her prayer and delivered a fantastic front end. Hal was friendly and enthused about her performance. It was as if they were performing together. Later, at class he told her she was powerful. She had pleased him. That made her feel good.

She noticed the same blonde woman accompanied him to the service and sat in the front row. Cynthia questioned someone in her prayer support group about this woman and was told that they were just friends. "She was friends of Hal and his ex-wife when he was married." Then the friend went on to explain something of Hal's background, "He studied for many years with another church. He's very intuitive and intelligent but he's had a hard life," she added.

The week of her forty-third birthday, Cynthia decided to buy the new car she had promised herself, if she did well after six months in Vancouver. It was a small white Buick. The morning the transaction was to take place, she became apprehensive and frightened about going through with the deal. Besides, the salesman who had promised to meet her at 1:00 p.m., had not shown up. Someone had told her that Hal had been a car salesman in his previous job and that he was the person to talk to. Since he had been supportive with her sprained ankle, she decided to reach out to him again.

She sat down teary-eyed in the dealership waiting for the salesman to arrive and complete the deal. She wept as the insurance man completed the transfer. The dealership cat gave her comfort, as she petted him. When she called Hal he said "Why don't you come down with your new car and we can go out for supper after?"

Was this a counseling session or a date? The call made her feel a lot better about the whole affair and she looked forward to seeing him. She parked the car on a side street near Broadway and walked to the centre.

"Hello, Cynthia," he said, and gave her the usual hug. "Come into my office." She sat down and he closed the door.

"So, you've bought a new car?" he asked.

"Right now I feel like quitting my job, so it seems so foolish to be buying a new car." The philosophy they were in, encouraged taking chances and not being overly cautious.

'Are you okay for money?" he ventured, "Could you get by for a while if you didn't work?"

He walked over to the window to smoke and blowing the smoke outside. Cynthia was against smoking, but she decided to overlook it for the time being. He then walked around the side of the desk to have a look at her legs.

"Yes'" she replied, "I do have some money from the sale of a condo. I could get by for a while." Right away she regretted saying it. But then again he was a minister. She should be able to trust him.

Then it was time to go to dinner. Again she was confused. Should she pay him for counseling or was this a date? As they left his office she noticed two photographs on his bookcase, one of Yogananda and the other of a small girl. She commented on the first and he filled her in on the second, "My daughter."

"She's beautiful," said Cynthia.

They then left to go to a Mexican restaurant where they decided to have the buffet. As they were filling their plates, Hal kept dropping things and fumbling with the food. She asked. "Am I making you nervous?"

During the conversation, she told him how she had come to move to Vancouver how she had used all the principles of New Thought to make it happen for her The philosophy included making a decision about what you want and then using prayer and affirmations to achieve it. She also told of how she had come to find her apartment, where cats were not only allowed but welcomed.

"Do you have cats?" he asked.

"I have one," she replied, forgetting to ask how he felt about them.

When they finished dinner, he insisted on paying and she took him to where she had parked her car. As she drove home, she still had the feeling the two of them were somehow connected. Once home she discovered her old lover had called and left a message on the machine.

Chapter Three: Release It!

On the actual day of Cynthia's forty-third birthday, Hal was holding the grand opening of his centre and all the participants were invited to attend. With no other plans, she dressed in a slinky black dress and drove into Vancouver. Hal was at the door greeting people with his daughter, a pretty little blonde girl of about five years old. When he saw Cynthia, he bent to kiss her, as well as giving her a hand shake. Confused about the meaning of this, she played it cool but friendly.

The evening turned out to be something of a disaster since one of the performers, who was supposed to play his flute, didn't show up until very late; and when he did, he came without the flute. He played the piano instead. The program was delayed, and time was wasted with silly games. Chantelle, Hal's daughter, behaved rather badly, looking at people through her legs with her bum toward them.

Cynthia left the celebration with the impression that Chantelle was very spoiled and the centre was not very organized. The blonde lady was nowhere to be seen until very late in the evening.

When Cynthia went to bed, she had Hal's kiss on her mind and during the night she had recurring dreams that she was calling his name. What the meaning of the dream was she didn't know but she felt somehow she was very connected to him.

In the weeks that followed, she told one of her friends about him. She never heard from him during the week and only saw him at class so she had no real clues that his interest in her was anything other than a teacher and a student. Also the blonde lady was somehow involved.

Then finally the pieces of the puzzle fell into place and Cynthia discovered the truth that this woman was living with Hal. How serious their relationship was she did not know. One thing she did know for sure was that she was not going to be another mistress to an attached man.

Hal's centre had another celebration for Thanksgiving and again Cynthia had no other plans so once again went, taking a salad. The centre provided the turkey dinner. This time the blonde woman was sitting next to Hal at the table and Cynthia saw how he affectionately touched her shoulder. Cynthia took it all in and decided that if a relationship between herself and Hal was meant to be then she would leave it alone and wait.

At home in bed as she often did, she asked for a dream that would provide the answer. This was her dream. She was going to a concert that was to begin at 8:00 p.m. When she got to the auditorium, there was no one there. She noticed the clock read 6:00 p.m. She waited. The room began to fill but was not yet full. The clock read 7:25. It was still not time. When she awoke, she knew the answer. It was not time yet! In the morning, she petted her beloved Siamese cat, Simba, who had come with her to this new place. "I love Simba so much but it is not enough, I need something more." she thought

Cynthia's energy turned to her work. She was not very happy with the way her employer did things and still thought and dreamed about having her own business. She began investigating buying a franchise. She realized that creating a satisfying career life might be just as challenging as waiting for a relationship to develop.

Meanwhile, she decided to give Hal one more chance to clarify his intentions toward her, as he still seemed to be flirting with her in class. On her day off, she invited him to lunch to pay him back for the dinner he had bought her. He agreed and they met at a hotel restaurant, which was convenient for both.

Once seated, things seemed comfortable, so Cynthia told him how she and her first husband had stayed at that hotel when they were courting and had registered as Mr. and Mrs. They had a chuckle over it and Cynthia wondered if she should have mentioned it since he was a minister.

The conversation seemed relaxed. At one point Cynthia told Hal about her mother, who always treated people with children with more respect than those without. Since she had no children, she always felt like she didn't matter to her mother. With a quick intuitive observation, Hal zeroed in on her painful spot. "You've always wanted children haven't you? I'll pray about it for you."

Suddenly she felt uncomfortable and changed the subject.

She decided to get around to the reason she had arranged this luncheon. As she took the bill and put it on her credit card, he thanked her.

She replied, "You took me out to dinner that night I bought my new car and I wanted to repay you. I was going to invite you to dinner but I wasn't sure if you were in a relationship or not. I wasn't sure how to handle it, so I decided on lunch."

He stammered, "Well, I am," He stopped then continued, "Sort of.... In a relationship."

He didn't say any more but Cynthia found herself losing some of the respect she had for him. It sounded as if he was in a relationship that he was not proud of. She had somehow believed him to be stronger than that.

When they left the restaurant, he walked her to her car and thanked her again. The whole situation, which a few moments ago was charged with energy, was now lifeless. As she drove home she made a clear decision to let the whole idea of a relationship with him go. Whatever situation he was in, she was confident he had the strength and the skills to get out of it by himself. Although disappointed, she put him out of her mind and proceeded with the plans she had for her life.

In the teaching of her church, New Thought or Science of Mind, there were five steps to prayer, or treatment, as they called it. First there was the recognition of the presence of God. Second, you affirmed your oneness with God. The third step was to state what you wanted. Number four was to give thanks. The last or fifth step was to release it or let it go and watch the results come. Cynthia had just done step five.

Chapter Four: The Shift in Consciousness

With Hal out of her mind, Cynthia proceeded to make plans for the rest of her life. She decided to buy a franchise and even the location was what she wanted, after looking at several. The franchise was a drapery store. Her own business would give her the control over her life that she needed, something she did not have in her current job. It would also take the place of the relationship she did not have or at least fill the hours with something interesting that was her own.

As far as her personal life was concerned, she decided to reach out to friends more. She got the phone numbers of women in her class to keep in touch with them. She asked the members of her prayer support group for dinner one Sunday, as she was still involved with the Surrey Centre. She accepted a position offered to her on their Board of Directors.

Hal's eight-week class had come to a close. On the last evening people were passing around a birthday card for him for everyone to sign. It was his fiftieth birthday. As it was presented to him, Cynthia noticed the blonde lady whose name was Linda. There was a one-week break from class then a new round of eight weeks would begin. Cynthia considered dropping out partly because of the distance and partly because the person she was travelling with had decided not to continue. She decided she would wait and see how she felt closer to the date. She realized the class was the only thing she did for herself besides work. Telling herself she would know the right answer when the time came, she let it go for the two weeks.

She waited for a lawyer to get back to her on the suitability and legalities of the franchise contract. On her own she decided the contract to be very much in favor of the franchisor that received all benefits while the franchisee did all the work and received a small salary after all the bills were paid. She did know the benefits of franchises from her own research, that they were known to be more successful than small independent businesses. The man selling the franchises kept phoning her to see if she had made a decision yet.

Finally she called the lawyer and he told her the contract was pretty standard and that all franchise contracts were much alike. He neither encouraged her nor discouraged her. She decided to make an offer on the store that was her first choice.

As soon as she told the salesman, he responded quickly and angrily that that store was gone. The only one left was her last choice, the one he seemed to be pushing on her. The plans for the rest of her life were on hold for now.

Meanwhile, she went to Hal's first class in the series and didn't pay her fee, as she still had thoughts of dropping out. As class began, Cynthia sensed something was different. At one point in the lecture he talked about his centre and himself undergoing a shift in consciousness. He even went so far as to say he had blown the whole place apart. People on his board and things had changed for him personally. The center was moving on to the next stage.

Cynthia didn't know what it all meant but she was still undecided about continuing with the class and what to do about the franchise. She told her old lover on the phone about the franchise, "You can't accept wieners when you have your heart set on steak."

She gave herself the next week to decide about the class. As soon as she got home from work, she knew she had to go. Nothing could have prevented her from going. When she arrived at the Center, she stepped into Hal's office to pay her fee. He said, "I'm so glad you're coming back. I just love you so much. Every time I see you my heart just goes like." He made a fluttering signal with his hand. Throughout the class she wondered what he meant and what his situation was.

She did not hear from him the next week. And she still had not made a decision about the franchise. On the morning of the class, she decided to phone Hal and ask him for direction. "I'm trying to make a business decision and I would like to talk to you." she said. "Would it be okay if I came a little early to talk to you?"

"Why don't we go for coffee or a drink after class and we can spend some time together?" he suggested. "Or do you have to be up really early in the morning?"

"No, that's one good thing about my job," said Cynthia, "I set my own hours and I hate being up early."

"I always had those kinds of jobs," he explained. "I am a night person too."

So they agreed to go for coffee after the class was over and she would tell him what was on her mind. She wondered what else they would talk about.

When the class ended, they waited for everyone to leave. Hal locked up and they made their way across the street to a restaurant frequented with young people. They walked through the chrome railings and flashing neon signs to their table. Hal had not eaten before class so he ordered a cup of coffee and a hamburger and Cynthia had her usual glass of white wine.

He started out by asking about her dilemma, the decision she needed to make. She explained as briefly as possible the franchise idea and how disappointed she was with the outcome.

He asked, "Do you know what Jewish business people say are the three most important things in business, LOCATION, LOCATION AND LOCATION."

She was surprised by his response but it confirmed what she already believed. If she couldn't have the location she wanted, she didn't want it at all.

He then asked her, "Why do you want to have your own business? It is a tremendous amount of work."

"I don't have anything else to do."

He pondered her answer and then changed the subject. "Would you like to go out for dinner on Sunday? I'm taking a group on a retreat on the weekend but will be back on Sunday afternoon."

"Don't you have someone in your life?" she asked.

"She moved out three weeks ago. I'm now celibate," he said.

"Celibacy can be very healing," she answered. "I'd love to go out for dinner with you on Sunday."

"I'll be back Sunday afternoon. I'll call you. Decide on a place and make a reservation."

Her heart leapt. Was this really happening? Was it time? Were her plans and prayers really being answered? She couldn't make any assumptions yet. It was too soon. All he was doing was asking for one date.

They began talking about their lives." I have been married twice and have a grown family from my first marriage and a five-year-old daughter from my second marriage. I was nineteen when I married the first time and my pregnant bride was sixteen."

"I didn't have any children in either of my marriages, but my second husband hated cats," she explained. "Do you like cats?" she asked.

"Yes, I do," he said.

"I just have Simba, a Siamese cat and I love her very much." Cynthia was relieved that she wouldn't have to worry about Simba in a relationship with Hal

After they finished their food and beverages, Hal walked Cynthia back to her car.

"I am going to start taking Mondays off. That's your day off isn't it? Maybe we can do some things together," he said. She agreed.

Before saying goodnight he said, "I didn't know you would be so beautiful. I had asked for many things but beauty wasn't one of them."

Then he kissed her goodnight She drove home, her heart on fire.

The next day she called the franchise salesman and told him she didn't want any of the locations he had offered her.

Chapter Five: The Date

When Cynthia decided to shelve any thoughts of a relationship with Hal, one of the things she wanted to do was to take a trip. A friend, who had finished her semester at university, had invited her to go to Hawaii. The trip was planned for the first week of December. Cynthia had no holidays coming, so she took a week's leave from her job.

At the same time she was very excited about her date with Hal. She told one of her friends, "I hope I don't blow it."

"Just be yourself," her friend had said.

Just be yourself. She said a silent prayer and decided not to worry. The weekend of the date she was very busy trying to complete some deals she was working on. It meant taking a couple of calls on the Sunday afternoon. She also wanted her apartment to be clean and tidy. She then needed time to decide what to wear. Hal came early, which was typical of him. Dressed in a dinner jacket, shirt and tie, he arrived with a small bouquet of flowers.

Simba greeted him at the door and he petted her on the head saying, "She loves you very much." Cynthia chose a long black skirt and a white satin blouse. They chatted for a few moments as he told her about the retreat and how he kept wishing she was there. She told him she made a reservation at the Italian restaurant in the neighborhood.

They left for the restaurant after a few minutes and he led her to his car, which was an old wreck. "When I was in the car business, I always had a demonstrator. When I left the car business, I bought my deceased father in law's car, just to have something to hop around in. I apologize for its condition, also for the smoke smell."

They ended up going to a German restaurant on the same street as the Italian. Cynthia ordered a glass of white wine and he, a glass of Perrier. He explained how he never drank any alcohol after having drunk a lot at one time. She assumed he was in Alcoholics Anonymous.

They shared lot of information about each other. He told her of how he had left the car business." After I made a decision on a Friday night that I would have to do something else with my life, I was fired on Monday morning. A friend had observed that the car business had kicked me out. I was no longer in the right consciousness to do that type of work."

The dinner went very well and Cynthia was convinced that being herself was what Hal wanted. She was impressed with his good manners at the table. She ordered a Vienna Schnitzel, and he ordered a similar dish.

They returned to her apartment after, where she made tea. They talked some more. He told her this was the first date he had gone on. She replied by saying, "You are lucky. Dates are usually a pain."

She was surprised by his next question, "Would you like to go steady with me?"

"That's an expression I haven't heard since I was a teenager!" she laughed.

She knew she wanted to have a relationship with him. It was as if she had known him and always loved him since their first meeting and perhaps before that. Yes," she answered, "I'll go steady with you."

They sat and kissed on the couch for a while "Maybe we can neck too." She laughed using another 1950's expression. He left early as she had agreed to work the next day on her day off and she was leaving on Friday for her holiday.

The next day Hal stopped to visit after work. He had been out to White Rock to see another minister about the possibility of joining forces. He sat with Cynthia on the couch. This time he mentioned Linda, the woman he had recently broken up with. "She was always after me, even when I was married. I knew her years ago in another church. The three month thing, when she moved in with me, was a mistake."

"How did you manage to break up with her? Wasn't she pretty clingy?" asked Cynthia.

"After I became clear I wanted a relationship with you, she started moving out. It was as simple as that. Do you know when I decided I wanted a relationship with you? It was the day we met for lunch at the Blue Boy."

Cynthia smiled. "That's the day I decided to release the idea of a relationship with you and get on with the rest of my life."

"It is wonderful how the law works," Hal observed.
They kissed and embraced. "Is there anything else you want to know about me?" He paused, "I've had a vasectomy."

Cynthia was disappointed by the discovery, but she tucked it away.

"I didn't want to have any more children with Gretchen." Cynthia assumed Gretchen was his ex.

One of Cynthia's goals as well as a relationship was to have a baby. At forty-three, she had still not put the idea out of her mind. She didn't say anything to Hal but decided to pray about it.

That week she would have one more class to attend before leaving on her trip. After the class, Cynthia and Hal returned to the same restaurant where he had asked her for the date. He told her that one of the things that he did a lot of was counseling and that many of his clients were women. He hoped she wouldn't mind women phoning him a lot about their problems. He wanted to know if she were the jealous type. She sensed he was a bit disappointed when she assured him she was not.

This was the last time they would be together until she returned from Hawaii. He said he would leave the right time for the physical side of their relationship up to her.

"I am nervous about it," she admitted.

"So am I."

The next evening she was busy completing orders for the store before she went away. Once home, the phone rang immediately. It was Hal. He said, "The service at my centre is over now. I just got home. One of the men said how young I looked. It must be my new relationship."

"Isn't that wonderful?", said Cynthia.

Cynthia told him she would call him as soon as she returned from her trip. The next day she rose early to catch the plane to Hawaii.

Chapter Six: Christmas

As many planned activities turn out, Cynthia's trip to Hawaii could be described as a huge disappointment. It poured rain everyday. At one point mid-week, she considered returning and checked out the fare to go home. But being a completer, she decided to stick it out and hoped things would change and the weather would clear up. Part of her had not wanted to leave Vancouver after starting a new relationship. She had known of many relationships that had ended on briefer separations and she refused to let herself have expectations about this one until she was more certain.

Cynthia had a mixed bag of emotions about her life in general. She realized that each time she had come to Hawaii, she had been longing for someone, even though she had not used that term. That was Hal's word, She had gone with a girlfriend and wishing she were with a certain man. One decision she had made was that she was not going on another holiday like this one. She knew the next trip would be with a partner, lover or husband.

The flight home seemed endless. After a lengthy wait in the airport, they finally boarded the plane and began a trip, which seemed to take forever. Once at the Vancouver Airport, they had to wait for the car park people to come and pick them up and take them to the place where the car was parked. Cynthia thought of phoning Hal to come and get them, but she thought he might be still at the Christmas party being held at his centre. After they reached the car, she had to drive her friend home and then drive another half hour to reach her apartment.

Once there she had to pet poor Simba, who had been on her own for a week with only the landlady to feed her. There was mail piled up, greetings for the festive season from many friends back home. Finally drained of energy, Cynthia picked up the phone to call Hal.

To her delight, he answered on the first ring. She told him about the disappointing trip. He told her about the party at the centre, which was a disappointment as well. Then he switched the conversation over to their relationship.

"One day last fall, a lady came to see me for counseling, he said, "I knew that I wanted her."

It took a moment before she realized that he was talking about her.

"The day you asked me for lunch, was the day I made my decision to have you."

After a twenty-minute chat, she burst out with what was on her mind. "Do you feel like coming over?" It was probably three o'clock in the morning.

"Do you want me to come?"

"Yes, more than anything, I thought of phoning you from the airport to come and get us."

"I was hoping you would call. I'll be right over. I'll bring my pajamas, some coffee, and muffins for the morning.

Cynthia was excited. Their relationship seemed complete after the misgivings she had on the trip home. It was not sexual desire she felt but the desire to get on with the relationship following the long delay. The sexual energy she felt during the trip drained away during the long hours of traveling and waiting.

She spent the next forty minutes reading her mail and petting Simba who had missed her terribly. Hal finally arrived with a bag of overnight gear. They kissed and embraced at the door. Because of the late hour they decided to go to bed immediately. Each seemed nervous, so Cynthia suggested, "We can just go to sleep. We don't have to do anything else." This did not seem to rest well with Hal so they proceeded to try to make love. That's what it was, trying.

To say that Cynthia was disappointed in their sexual pursuits was an understatement. In addition to her losing all interest in sex on the way home, he had a similar experience. The Christmas party at the centre had done the same thing to him. A certain woman had hugged him and when she did he felt like he had lost all his power. Once in bed, he was unable to maintain an erection and could not reach an orgasm. Cynthia, who knew she was a sexually responsive woman, did climax a couple of times and was insulted when he told her he couldn't tell if she had or not. The long and short of it all appeared that they were not sexually compatible at all. Cynthia felt let down but decided that first times were often unsuccessful and she remained optimistic about the future. It must have been five a.m. when they finally fell asleep.

It was noon or later when they awoke. The day was spent lounging, talking, sharing life stories and for Hal smoking out the window. They drank coffee and ate muffins. Simba was truly insulted that someone had replaced her for her mother's affection. After being left alone for a week she expected to have all kinds of attention and now to be robbed of it again.

Cynthia shared her life stories with Hal, something she vowed she would never do again. She found that stories come back to haunt you. In any case, she told him about her marriages, her relationship with a married man, her lost pregnancies and other painful events.

Hal shared information about his first marriage and how after three children and a lot of guilt and anger, "We split up. My second wife, Gretchen, had worked for me and was my best sales person in the real estate office. A week after I left Jane, Gretchen made a play for me even though she was married. After a one-night stand, she moved in with me. We were married after I got a divorce from Jane."

"When did you have Chantelle?" asked Cynthia.

"We were married a long time before she got pregnant. I was a heavy drinker. It was after I quit drinking that she finally got pregnant. Then after she had Chantelle, she didn't want me anymore. He became introspective." You know, you are the first woman I have ever chosen. I had to marry Jane. Then Gretchen and Linda both picked me. It's different when you do the choosing."

The topic of Christmas came up. Cynthia had two invitations. "What are you going to do?" asked Cynthia.

"I could go to my folks place in Abbottsford." Hal replied.

Neither seemed enthused about their plans. Finally he asked, "Would you like to spend Christmas with me?"

"I thought you would never ask," replied Cynthia. They

decided to cook a small turkey at his apartment and she would prepare dessert. On Christmas Eve his center was having a late evening service so they decided Cynthia would stay over at his place after the service and be there for Christmas Day. She was happy to be spending the festive day with him but had many questions on her mind.

The Christmas Eve service didn't go well as Linda turned up and made Hal nervous. Cynthia wondered if he was truly over her. They got to bed late, around one thirty and woke up late. Cynthia wished she could have brought dear little Simba, but had left the land lady to feed her.

They cooked their turkey. Hal basted it with a mustard sauce while Cynthia prepared an English Christmas pudding. They ate their dinner and went for a long walk in the area of Vancouver where Hal lived. Then they spent some time lying around listening to Christmas music. They didn't try to make love and Cynthia wondered again if Hal could, or if there was a problem. At the end of the day Cynthia packed her bag to go home, as she had to go to work on Boxing Day. She had some melancholy emotions like she was being let down. Simba was very happy to see her and the reverse was true, also.

She was at home for a short time on Boxing Day during which Hal dropped by with Chantelle. He was taking her to his mother's place for her Christmas visit. He also wanted her to meet Cynthia, as they had not officially met that night at the center. At that point she seemed like a pleasant, nice little girl. He had told Chantelle that Cynthia was his girlfriend.

Chapter Seven: Winter's Lull

Cynthia was full of questions after spending Christmas alone with Hal. In many ways their relationship was a match. In others ways, it didn't seem to work at all. He seemed more content with it than she did. She recalled one evening in his class when he talked about a perfect relationship being right physically, emotionally, intellectually and spiritually. She tried to evaluate theirs on this framework. Most relationships are good emotionally and physically only and then they burn out. Cynthia's relationship with Hal in her opinion was high on spiritual and intellectual. Their spiritual beliefs were so similar and they seemed connected at a deep level, often thinking of the same thought at the same time.

Intellectually, they could discuss anything and had the same interests. She remembered one day when he asked her, "Do you like camping?"

She replied, "I hate camping. "

He looked relieved, "That's wonderful," he replied. "Gretchen always wanted to go camping and I had to struggle to keep from going. That's what I like about my relationship with you. Everything is easy."

It was the physical or sexual side of their relationship that bothered Cynthia. At first Hal was nonfunctional and accused Cynthia of being too passive sexually. Then he decided to think it over and came up with the conclusion that he had always been too controlling, coming from his ego in his previous sexual relationships with Gretchen and Linda. He decided to surrender sexually rather than trying to be in control. After that, it was better, but Cynthia still found sex with him cumbersome and awkward. He was always talking about his sex life with Linda, which made Cynthia ill at ease. To top it off, he would accuse her of talking about her previous sexual partners, of whom he was jealous. Cynthia wished at times that they could just be friends.

It was also the emotional side of their relationship she felt was not right. She did not feel overly excited or passionate, but conversely she did not feel negative emotions such as jealousy or anger, at least not at this early stage of the relationship.

Hal's children were a problem. Because they were a problem for him, they became a problem for Cynthia. The young daughter, Chantelle, started out as interesting in the relationship but as time went on became increasingly more of a challenge. Chantelle was very spoiled. Hal paid quite a lot of child support and was supposed to have custody every second weekend. This rarely happened as Gretchen, his ex, seemed to be in complete control to change plans whenever she pleased. Hal's three older grown children were not a problem as he mostly ignored them. Chantelle was everything and they were nothing. The eldest daughter, Tracey, particularly disliked him. Cynthia was not sure of the reason. His second daughter, Janine and his son, Tim wanted his attention but didn't get it.

Another problem was money. Hal confided in Cynthia that he had no money. In fact he had debts. This did not sit right with her but on the other hand, her last husband had lots of money but did not share any with her. She felt Hal had the potential to make money so in her mind the problem was solvable.

Cynthia disliked the way Hal "babied" people who had problems, particularly women, from his centre. He kept insisting that they needed his help. It seemed to Cynthia they were leeches draining him of energy, but he liked it.

In spite of all the things that bothered her about him, Cynthia felt that Hal loved her. One day she was walking Simba outside when he arrived. His face beamed, an adoring smile, when he saw her. She somehow felt her life was better with him than without. She also felt that he could be a better person with her in his life.

When they had time away from the centre life, which was rare, they spent time talking, which pleased Cynthia as she enjoyed conversation. Their interests were the same as they were a pair of couch potatoes who spent time discussing God, the world and humanity.

During the week, Cynthia was busy with her job. They saw each other on Wednesday evening for class and on weekends, when Cynthia would usually stay over on Saturday night and go to church with Hal on Sunday mornings. On Sunday afternoons they would relax together.

A couple of times Hal was invited to speak at churches in Victoria, so they caught the ferry to Vancouver Island. Cynthia enjoyed the trip over to the island and meeting new spiritual people. She felt that she belonged in this life.

The one church in particular was friendly and the winter day was warm and sunny and embracing. She and Hal seemed to belong together as the gulls swooped down on the beach.

Cynthia felt very content with her life. She didn't realize it but this was a sort of lull before a storm.

Chapter Eight: The Engagement

January and February progressed and so did the relationship between Hal and Cynthia with a few minor problems or so it seemed to Cynthia. After they returned from one of their trips to Victoria, they stopped for something to eat and Hal accidentally called her "Linda." If this was a Freudian slip, then he couldn't think very highly of her since he was always referring to Linda as wimpy, weak and manipulative. On the other hand, he was always telling Cynthia how much he admired her for her ability to express herself and speak publicly. Cynthia was confused, but she didn't confront him about it.

One Sunday evening after he had taken Chantelle home, he stopped at Cynthia's apartment for a short visit. He appeared restless. He referred to the first time she had come to his center.

"You seemed to have a problem you needed help with," he said.

Cynthia was again confused unable to think of a problem." I can't recall a problem," she replied. Then they got on the topic of relationships. "I have always found controlling men the greatest problem in all my relationships." she observed.

He came back with, "It is always the ones who find controlling partners a problem who are the worst controllers themselves."

She was taken by surprise by his rudeness but said only, "You could be right."

He lay down on the couch with his head in her lap, all the while shifting about, and complaining about being uncomfortable.

Finally he said, "I better be going, as I have classes tomorrow."

Cynthia knew he had no classes before afternoon, and probably not before evening. She was disappointed but didn't object. He got up and prepared to leave. They said their goodnights to each other in a disconcerting way and he left.

She decided if this was the end of their relationship it was fine, that she had not done anything to end it. She had not yet begun to connect his talking to Gretchen with his moodiness and negativity. She would go to class on Wednesday and play it by ear.

Wednesday night finally came. Cynthia wondered what to expect. Would Hal treat her like he had when she was a student or would he treat her like she was his lover? As she walked into the center Hal acted as if nothing had happened between them. As soon as he saw her, he said warmly. "Hi Honey" and embraced her. Their relationship carried on as usual.

Another time when Hal's personality was unpredictable was one evening when they were eating dinner at his apartment. Hal was telling Cynthia how good she was at speaking and writing. Without thinking Cynthia blurted out, "Maybe we can do something together sometime in terms of a center,"

To Cynthia's surprise Hal leapt from the dinner table shouting, "No I can't work with anyone! I have to work alone. You have to understand that." He sat down again, leaving his knife and fork where they lay.

Cynthia remained silent. She was puzzled. She knew the statement he had just made was not true as he already had Jesse, the woman he had recruited from the Surrey Church, working for him. Cynthia realized her suggestion must have threatened him big time. She also knew that he could be wrong, that if they were intended to work together then nothing could stop it from happening. They finished eating in silence. Later he accused Cynthia of being in a "funny" mood. She wondered who was in the funny mood.

For the most part, he was affectionate and supportive in their times together. They didn't talk about their difficult times but tended to ignore them. Cynthia wondered if she brought them up would he show the anger he had at the table that night. She felt happy most of the time about the relationship and safe as if she were not alone in the world. She had something in life beside her

31

work.

The winter passed and the month of February came and went. It turned out to be that "one in four" or in other words "leap year" when February has twenty-nine days. Cynthia happened to be at Hal's center on that day. Everyone was talking about it being the day when women propose marriage and couples become engaged. People were laughing and deciding on where to go for lunch. Hal and Cynthia had no real plans for lunch when he asked, "Why don't we go to the Granville Island Hotel, honey?"

"Sounds great!" replied Cynthia

It was a kind of trendy old hotel on Grandville Island and they drove over there and parked her car as usual. Once seated, they ordered drinks. They started talking about marriage. In the past they had assumed it would happen for them at some point in the future but no dates were discussed.

Hal said "I would ask you to marry me today but I'm afraid of rejection."

Cynthia answered, "I am not afraid of rejection, I am afraid of commitment."

Hal said, "Well, I am not afraid of commitment."

Cynthia in her boldest voice said, "Why don't I ask you, because I am not afraid of rejection" They then agreed.

Before Cynthia could object or think it over, she asked, "Hal, I love you and I would like to marry you. Will you marry me?"

"I love you too. And I accept." Hal's face was beaming with joy.

They then went back to the center and announced their engagement to their friends and people at the centre. For the most part, Cynthia felt good about it, but there was a small twitch in the pit of her stomach. She had just become engaged to a man of many moods.

Chapter Nine: Wedding Plans, Changes and Moving Ahead

Cynthia was elated about her engagement as if this were her first. Hal publicly apologized for not being able to afford a ring. Did he arouse the sympathy he sought?

They got around to telling friends and family. Cynthia's family was a little wary, wondering if she shouldn't be a little more careful. Hal's mother, a religious Mennonite, was downright rude and confronted him on ruining two families and women's lives already, Was he going to try a third? "Are you going to have more children? Oh, that's right. You had an operation." She paused. "I suppose she has black hair." (All her relatives were blonde Mennonites) "You can't expect us to support you in this."

Their wedding date was the subject of much of their conversation over the next few weeks. Cynthia wanted to be married in an outdoor park. They decided upon a date early in June. Hal, much to Cynthia's surprise brought up the topic of children. Cynthia had actually put the idea out of her mind, for various reasons, age being one of them.

"I know how much this means to you. "He said. "I am going to see a doctor to find out about having the vasectomy reversed.

"When men have vasectomies, it usually means that is their final decision." said Cynthia "Why did you have it done in the first place?"

"I didn't want to have any more children with Gretchen. Did

you know you are the only woman I have ever wanted to have children with?"

Cynthia left the vasectomy topic with him, letting him know she was ambivalent. In a week or ten days, he got back to her that he had seen a doctor and the prognosis was that there was a 50/50 chance of the vasectomy reversal being a success. She wondered if a doctor's consultation could be obtained in such a short time. The other part of the news was that the cost was $1,800.00. Guess whose pocket that would come out of?

"Let's wait until our wedding day and make the decision then," said Hal closing the topic for further discussion.

Meanwhile things were happening at Hal's centre. He began having disagreements with Jesse, the large woman he had drawn away from the Surrey church. Cynthia stayed out of it as much as possible but when questioned about her opinion of Jesse's assets to the church, Cynthia did not see Jesse as a person of value. Hal must have listened to Cynthia because the next day he fired her. It turned out that many of the people from the centre took sides with Jesse. Because of the dissention in the church, Hal later came to blame Cynthia for the whole problem. But that would come much later.

In addition to the congregation falling away, Hal received a letter from the landlord that the building was slated for demolition in September He phoned Cynthia in almost a panic.

"What are we going to do? You and I are planning to create our own center in September. How are we going to pay the rent on the place until then?"

Wondering if he was expecting her to offer to pay the five months' rent, she adamantly in her mind refused and became perfectly clear that she was not coming up with one penny.

"Don't pay it. Let the building go. The centre is bringing in very little money and half of the people have quit. Close it"

"You're right! He said after a moment of thought. "That centre is my lack and limitation. Those people are a bunch of losers. I'll announce it tomorrow. I'll start looking for a job and we'll plan to start our own center in the fall."

Cynthia couldn't believe her ears. This was exactly what she wanted to hear. A final goodbye service was planned for the following Sunday by some of the flock who remained in the church.

It happened that Hal had reconciled in part with his mother and she had decided to accept his third marriage and his third wife. That meant that Cynthia had to go out to Abbottsford to meet her future in-laws. The big event was planned for a Sunday dinner.

Cynthia was working the Saturday before and came home to find Hal waiting for her outside her apartment. He came in with her. Just then her friend Harriett stopped by for a visit. Hal grinned and addressed Cynthia, "Chantelle is going with us tomorrow, and so is Tim." Tim was his son. Because Harriett was there, Cynthia could not object, but was fuming inside.

Harriet stayed only a short time. Then Cynthia spoke her mind.

"You didn't ask me if Tim and Chantelle could go to your mother's with us. I'm meeting your parents for the first time and you are taking them along."

"They never get to see my folks, "he stammered. Then he picked up the phone and dialed someone and said "I won't be taking Chantelle tomorrow. It's not convenient." Then he hung up. Cynthia guessed it was Gretchen. It had been her idea,

Hal sat down on the couch. Cynthia sat down on a chair.

"Oh, I had a terrible day at work," she continued. "All my orders were mixed up. I hate that job."

"YOU HATE EVERY JOB!" he roared." EVERY JOB IS JUST A RE-CREATION OF YOUR FAMILY. YOU CREATE YOUR FAMILY WHEREVER YOU GO. YOU ARE NOT CAPABLE OF ANYTHING ELSE.",

Silence from the couch. Cynthia couldn't believe what she was hearing; he had always spoken to her softly and gently in the past.

He continued. "AND I CAN'T TAKE MY KIDS TO VISIT MY PARENTS. I HAVE TO ASK YOU FIRST."

"This is the first time I am meeting them, didn't you think about that?" asked Cynthia

"IT WAS JUST BANG, LIKE THAT," he raged. "GRETCHEN WOULD NEVER HAVE DONE ANYTHING LIKE THAT!"

They sat there staring at each other for a while.

Finally she said, "Where's the unconditional love?"

More silence. The next morning was the final closing service at his centre. It was supposed to be a celebration. Hal finally got up and walked out the door.

Cynthia couldn't think of anything she had done wrong. Maybe their engagement was over. If so, so be it. She got ready for bed when the phone rang. It was Hal. He was remorseful but not apologetic.

"Are you coming to the centre tomorrow morning?"

"No," she answered and hung up.

She slept surprisingly well. She awakened to the ring of the phone again. It was Hal again. This time he was in a begging tone and sweet talking mode. After all, what would the people of the church think if she, his fiancée, was not there on the closing day of the church? Finally, Cynthia relented, as he knew she would and she hurried to get ready.

Sunday dinner at Abbotsford was very boring. Hals folks were sort of placid, people whom she knew were evaluating her by what terms she knew not. She was to discover in time a tangled web of phoniness lurked in the whole group. She knew she wasn't being compared to either of Hal's previous wives because they hadn't liked them either. They disapproved of everything he did.

His Mother at one point said, "I thought Chantelle might come." Cynthia knew that word had gotten around.

Cynthia had won for the moment and the storm was over for the time being, but there was a lot on the agenda yet.

Chapter Ten: Be Careful What You Pray For

Hal and Cynthia found themselves in the precarious situation of being unemployed and living together. They had set their wedding date for June the fifth and planned to start another church in the fall. In the meantime they taught a few seminars in the evenings on positive living and spiritual growth mostly to friends. Cynthia had given up her job at the department store, as she grew tired of her orders being messed up and customers complaining, so she decided to collect unemployment until they could start their church. Hal had closed his centre in Vancouver and would re-invent himself with Cynthia.

Hal had no money of his own and was unable to borrow any so one day he approached Cynthia. "I'd like to talk to you. What do think of you borrowing some money, say $5000? Then we'd have some capital to work with to start our centre. We could start running some courses and evening workshops right away. We could rent some space until such time as we are ready to open the church in the fall"

Cynthia, who had never borrowed money in her life, nearly flipped out of her chair.

"We could go to your bank manager where you have an excellent credit rating and of course pay it back on time each month. It would give us some money to work with."

"Of course it would have to be paid back on a regular basis," said Cynthia. Before she realized it she had been conned into going to her bank manager to ask for a loan. She did it, but was not comfortable with the idea. Going to the bank she felt like she was walking on eggs, not knowing what the future had in store for her. She knew she loved Hal and had confidence in what he had planned for them. To ease her discomfort with the whole idea, she made a joke about how they could abscond with the bank's money.

They looked at venues for their potential centre and sat down making lists of what they needed in terms of furniture and books. Hal itemized the following, "A location, one hundred chairs, a piano, song books, and a podium." They would then do prayer, asking for all the things they needed. They would use the five steps of treatment that they learned in their teaching, releasing it to God to provide to them. Cynthia had not a clue where any of it would come from, but she had received other answers to prayer and so her faith remained solid.

One other thing Cynthia was sure of was that she was not going to marry an unemployed man. She told Hal that. He went out looking for jobs in the car business where he had been employed in the past. However, to no avail. Cynthia felt sorry for him, a spiritual man having to look for employment in a business that ripped people off for a living. So she eased up on him but kept her desire not to marry someone unemployed.

They made their wedding plans; they were going to have everything decorated in pink and blue. He even asked her at one point if she wanted to post pone their wedding or call it off altogether. He saw her despondency, when the telephone company added his unpaid bill to hers. She had never had anything like this happen to her before in her life. The banks held all his cheques for three banking days before they cashed them. Could love prevail over all this?

With things not going well financially, Chantelle getting on Cynthia's nerves, they decided to get a weekend away. Taking the ferry over to Victoria to visit Richard a fellow minister sounded like a great idea. Cynthia enjoyed sipping wine while sitting at a café in the inner harbour. The trip was very relaxing and took their minds off all their worries.

When they returned home on Sunday evening, there was a call from Grace at the Surrey Church.

"Oh-oh! I haven't paid the rent on the chairs I borrowed

from them," speculated Hal.

"Here we go again," thought Cynthia. "More unpaid bills."

After a bit Hal returned Grace's call. He spoke to her for quite a few minutes. Obviously, it wasn't the chairs they were talking about. When he finally hung up, Cynthia's curiosity was sufficiently aroused.

"The minister they hired to replace Bonnie and Bill can't seem to get a work visa here in Canada. He has to go back to the States. Rather than start all over again interviewing candidates, they are offering me the job, since I am without a church at this time."

"There it is Hal, the answer to our prayers, a location, a congregation, one hundred chairs, song books, a podium, a piano, the whole bit." exclaimed Cynthia.

"And we don't have to wait until fall. They want us to start right away," said Hal

The answer to Cynthia's other prayer, not to marry a man who was unemployed was also answered as the new church was to open on June 5, their wedding day.

Chapter 11: Step Parenting, Sex and

Cigarettes

Cynthia enjoyed feeling like she had a family, friends and acquaintances would ask if she and Hal were going to have a family. This was something she had never had. As their wedding day came closer she knew she and Hal having a baby together was not going to happen. It would be like having two babies to take care for. She spoke to Hal about it and told him her decision. They were both disappointed, but understood that the reasons were sensible. At first she hoped she, Chantelle and Hal could be a family but the problem was Chantelle. It seemed that whatever custody agreement Hal had with Gretchen, it was never adhered to. Gretchen wanted to control it. She was always doing something that changed it and her word was always the law.

The other difficulty was that Chantelle was a little spoiled brat and Hal refused to discipline her. She was constantly hurting herself and then screaming for what seemed like hours, trying to get and hold her father's attention. When he told her to go to bed she would cry and scream, "I don't want to go to bed". Then he would let her stay up longer. The crying and screaming made everything very tense, especially for Cynthia. If Cynthia told Chantelle to do something, she would say, "no," and Hal would let her away with it.

One day when they went to visit Hal's parents, Chantelle began slapping Hal's father (an eighty year old man with a heart condition) on the back as hard as she could. Hal just sat there and said nothing. Chantelle would tease and annoy Simba, dragging her on her leash. Cynthia had to intervene on more than one occasion. Chantelle would refuse to eat her meals and would leave the table before everyone was finished to watch television or play.

It bothered Cynthia that Hal spoke to Chantelle in the same tone of voice as he did to herself, Cynthia. If Chantelle needed disciplining Hal accused Cynthia of being jealous of Chantelle, of treating her like Cynthia's younger sister, May, whom her father had favored. Cynthia had shared some childhood secrets with Hal and he would use them to undermine her. In order to avoid disciplining his precious child, he would lay the blame on Cynthia, who would wonder if she was going insane.

"You're jealous of her!" He would shout at her. "You can't stand to see me have a relationship with my little daughter. Just like your sister and your dad. You want me to be after her all the time."

"I do not. I just want her to behave so she doesn't drive us crazy." But secretly, Cynthia questioned her own motives. Maybe she was jealous of Chantelle. She didn't think so, but Hal brought up old feelings of shame and guilt that went back to childhood and her sister. In her stronger moments, she was sure that Chantelle reminded her of badly behaved spoiled children from school when she had been a teacher. She tried to make Chantelle's visits pleasant by buying colouring books and paper doll sets to play with.

Gretchen would phone any time day or night to change plans for Chantelle and expect them to change theirs. One day, Hal and Cynthia were invited to dinner at Betty's place for 6:00 p.m. Gretchen called to say that Chantelle had to be as a birthday party from 5:00 to 6:00.

Hal said, "Call Betty and tell her we will be late."

Cynthia said, "No, Hal, you tell Gretchen that we have made previous commitment and Chantelle will have to leave the birthday party early so we can get there on time." He did so reluctantly and Cynthia could tell he wasn't used to disobeying Gretchen.

Something else Cynthia pondered during their courtship was Hal's interest in other women. He always gave the impression that he adored Cynthia and found her the most attractive woman in the world. However, a few days before the wedding when the Church board was making arrangements to transfer the church over to Hal and Cynthia, there was a young attractive woman present at the church who had been the treasurer. Hal was clearly flirting with her and she with him. This made Cynthia very uncomfortable. When the minister came to go over the marriage service with Hal and Cynthia, Hal dismissed her and Cynthia, saying he had to review something with the treasurer. Cynthia was angry and wished she had spoken her displeasure and insisted that he be present with the minister and herself. After all, it was his wedding too.

As time went on, after their marriage, women kept popping up that Hal was clearly attracted to, some were married, some were single, all were weak personalities and if Cynthia mentioned it to Hal he would say they had come to him for counseling or he would accuse her of being jealous. None of these women measured up to Cynthia in any way, but Hal found them places in the Church. They had nothing for Cynthia to be jealous of and yet a tingling uneasy feeling remained with her.

One day Cynthia mentioned to a friend that she was disturbed by Hal's mishandling of money. The friend had then commented, "At least you are getting some sex." Cynthia then realized she was not satisfied with her sexual relationship with Hal although he claimed to be satisfied and thought it to be wonderful. For one thing he often wanted oral sex. He loved it. Cynthia enjoyed intercourse. She found it a complete act of fulfillment. Hal was very slow to reach orgasm. Sometimes Cynthia could have many orgasms to his one. He was always wanting to be told how good he was and how he was the best. Cynthia did not want to lie.

Cynthia did not feel the same need to have her sexual performance rated. Hal was always telling Cynthia how good his previous relationship, Linda, was at oral sex. As time went on Cynthia came to dread sex. She mistook it for being satisfied. At least that is what she told herself, that she was satisfied sexually. After a time, she realized that she was not satisfied.

On her list of what traits she wanted in a man was "nonsmoker." People would then ask her how she coped with Hal's smoking. When Cynthia went to Hal's office for the first time, he had smoked out the window. He never smoked in their apartment. Still the smell of cigarettes bothered her. She had

42

accepted him as a smoker, now she had to deal with it. One time, he had barely enough money for a package of cigarettes, yet he spent the money on it. Once he gave up smoking for five days and then went back on it. She was enabling him. She knew that. What would it take to make him a nonsmoker? In the relationship seminars which Hal and Cynthia taught, one principle was that what you see is what you get. You can't change anyone. So in the end she had to accept Hal's smoking. Or did she?

Chapter 12: The Wedding

Cynthia woke up on the morning of June 5, to her two-fold dream being answered. It was the day of their wedding and their new church opening. Hal began his new job as minister and Cynthia was the M.C. She got up early to go to the hairdresser.. In spite of a heated argument a few days beforehand about smoking, the ceremony actually took place on June 5, 1988.

The guest list had been compiled without too much dissent. Cynthia's family had arrived from Alberta a couple of days before. Hal's family had agreed to come although they had been against the marriage to begin with. The ceremony was to take place in a lovely park, called the Friendship Garden in New Westminster and a musician had been hired to play his flute.

Pink was Cynthia's favorite colour. (Hal had promised to plant pink flowers all around their home if they ever had one.) So of course she chose pink lace for her wedding dress with a small 1940's hat. All the flowers were of course pink. Hal rented a light blue tuxedo with a pink cummerbund and bow tie. They were well attired, a pink disaster, but that is what they wanted.

The hotel where the reception was to be held was decorated with pink and blue flowers, Chantelle and Carmen, Cynthia's little niece wore matching pink and white dresses with flower baskets in pink and white.

As the four entered the park, the flutist played beautiful music. A female New Thought minister had been hired to do the ceremony at 2:00 pm; Wedding party and guests waited and waited. Finally Hal left the park to phone her, pre cell phone days.

It turned out she thought the service was an hour later. However, she did arrive and delivered a lovely modern day exchange of vows while the two little girls were throwing sticks and hit a wedding guest in the head.

The wedding party then moved to the hotel. The minister continued her series of mistakes. "Where do you want me to sit?" she asked Cynthia, after informing Cynthia she would not be attending.

"I don't care where you sit," replied a disgusted Cynthia.

Thinking the minister wasn't coming; an alternate person was selected to say the grace. As soon as it was over the minister jumped up and said the longest grace in history.

The dinner of baked salmon was delicious and the flute player proved himself to be just as creative on the piano. They served both alcoholic and nonalcoholic punch for those who didn't drink. When it came time to toast the bride, Hal gave a ridiculously flowery reply. He rambled on about "this wonderful woman has changed my life in such a positive way. I am so wondrously blessed and so thankful to God for this gift."

He then went on about the church, which he called "our ministry, God has blessed us and blessed me with the gift of a partner."

Cynthia thought that he would never stop and felt embarrassed since many of the guests were not churchgoers.

Cynthia's gift was the "bill" and the sense of apprehension that went with it, in the pit of her stomach and in her pocket book.

Chantelle managed to spit on some of the wedding guests.

After the reception was over, everyone thanked them and wished them well. Hal insisted they open all their gifts when they got back to their apartment. Many of them were envelopes of money, so Hal stuffed some larger bills into his pocket. All the money he had for the honeymoon was fifty dollars his mother had given him. Cynthia always felt sorry for him when he got so excited about gifts as if he never had any as a child.

Then they started out for Harrison Hot Springs in Cynthia's car where they were to spend two or three days for their honeymoon. It was dark when they arrived. They went to their room and undressed. Hal poured a glass of Champagne for Cynthia and Perrier for himself.

Cynthia felt blissful. The day was perfect almost. She felt

she loved Hal and that everything should go well from now on. Hal must have felt the same way, because he said, "I love you very much. I am so grateful." He didn't say happy. He never said happy.

It was late when they went to bed. Sex was wonderful. There was no oral sex. Cynthia had multiple orgasms. She fell asleep from exhaustion.

Chapter 13: Bill and Bonnie

The next morning Hal made what Cynthia considered a strange and unexpected comment. But perhaps it was not that way to him. Maybe he was being honest for once in his life.

He said, "I hope I can always be faithful to you."

She replied, after some hesitation, "If I can't be faithful to you, I would end the relationship first".

He said "If we are ever going to end our relationship, let's only end it when it's good, not when it's bad."

She didn't know what he meant by that.

On the way back to Vancouver, they talked about the work that lay ahead with the church. Simba was waiting for them at the apartment along with all the unwrapped gifts and paper.

They realized how they had stepped into the shoes of the couple, Bill and Bonnie, who had returned to California the summer before. The congregation regarded them in the same light, as "Mom and Dad." On Sundays Cynthia began the service with the opening prayer, announcements and then introduced Hal, who then gave a sermon or lecture. The service ended with a closing prayer and coffee.

As well as Sunday services, they taught a few classes during the week on various topics such as prosperity, relationships with a handful of people in attendance. This continued through the summer.

Their relationship remained fairly stable. Usually Hal was a wonderful friend to Cynthia as they discussed how they were growing and overcoming old self-defeating behavior.

Other times, he was moody and did things, which made her, feel afraid. Once he broke a plaque she had bought in Spain, only she could have sworn he did it on purpose, just to annoy her. Another time a cheque from one of the students for a course, had disappeared. After searching all over for it, Cynthia found it on the lower shelf of the bookcase. Only Hal could have put it there. He denied having done it and accused her. Another time the key to the storage room disappeared. Cynthia searched every possible place and finally found it in the bottom of the garbage under a lot of paper. Hal again denied having put it there and almost accused Cynthia of being crazy. When he realized these acts didn't faze her, he stopped doing them.

Over the summer months, money was scarce. Hal enjoyed calling Cynthia a MISER when she didn't want to pay for a lot of expensive things that he could not afford, such as meals out. At first she felt guilty and paid for some of them but after a time when he called her a miser or a cheapskate, she agreed with him. "Yes, I am a miser and I am going to stay that way."

Attendance at the church was low and therefore collections were down. Cynthia was receiving unemployment insurance and Hal had asked the church for a commission rather than a salary so low collections meant low pay. Gretchen, of course demanded a full amount of child support, including tuition for tap dancing lessons.

Even though Cynthia was supposed to be happy, doing what she wanted with the person she wanted, she felt stressed. The weekends when Chantelle came were stressful since Hal insisted on spoiling her. Gretchen was always complaining that he wasn't taking her enough. Cynthia felt stress from having to perform on Sunday mornings from writing prayers, talks, teaching classes, from helping Hal with his sermons since he had only a Grade nine education. She was stressed by his moods and his insistence that they visit his parents every two weeks. There it was evident that Gretchen had been influencing his mother that they were not taking Chantelle enough. Cynthia wondered where her life was in all of this.

Meanwhile back at the church there was the treasurer, Sandra, who was a married woman with three kids. Hal was still making googly-eyes at her. She seemed to reciprocate, always trying to get him alone making appointments for counseling and such. Whenever Hal mentioned her name he became starry-eyed like he was drunk. It was time she did something about it, Cynthia decided.

On Sunday afternoons they always went for a picnic at the Friendship Garden. This is where they always talked about "things."

"Okay," she said, "this won't go away, so I am going to say it. You are going to have to do something about your addiction to Sandra Hays!"

"Oh I think she reminds me of Tracey, my oldest daughter," he stammered. "Her feet are the same."

At least he didn't accuse Cynthia of being jealous of Sandra or being crazy.

At a time when Cynthia should or felt she should feel relaxed and enjoying the work at the church, which was what she really wanted to do, she felt stressed. She felt that her worries were not over just because Hal had a job, and that she was somehow unappreciated and uneasy.

Chapter 14: House and Home

Hal and Cynthia felt certain that fall with people returning from vacations would mean people back in church. Classes in personal and spiritual growth should be overflowing with those anxious to get back to work and prosper. Cynthia believed very strongly that their prayers would be answered this time as in the past. All they could do was wait and trust in the infinite power that was supplying all of their needs. There was however, some doubt in Cynthia's mind, since she could not control Hal's mind or what he was thinking.

In the evenings when they weren't planning lectures and prayers, they would go for walks in the lush foliage of New Westminster and look at houses. They would discuss the various features they liked and disliked about the houses they saw on their route. Older style homes with dormer windows seemed to catch their eyes. They did the same thing when they drove around spotting condos for sale, wondering if any were within their price range.

At home they made lists of features they wanted in a home. Since they both liked coffee first thing in the morning, they decided jokingly, a coffee alcove in the bedroom, as a must. A large master bedroom with an ensuite bath was another must. Neither cared if the house had a fireplace or not.

Hal had not forgotten that pink was Cynthia's favorite colour, so he planned that wherever they lived, he would plant pink flowers all around their home, especially pink roses.

One day they noticed a small bungalow for sale up the

street from their apartment. An elderly couple had placed it for sale independently of a realtor. The couple's middle-aged daughter was showing it for them. Hal and Cynthia called her and made arrangements to view it. Hal said to Cynthia, "Let me do the talking." In his car salesman voice, he explained how they were just starting the church and probably wouldn't qualify for a bank mortgage. He then offered the woman a price and asked if her parents would consider financing them.

The woman checked back with her parents and of course called back to refuse the conditions of the deal. Cynthia said, "I could have told you so." The house needed a lot of work and repairs so they weren't terribly disappointed.

Grace, from the church was a realtor, so they asked her to show them another house, which they found interesting. It was very large and needed a lot of work. It would have taken all of Cynthia's money for the down payment. With utilities, mortgage payments and other expenses, it would clean them right out. Cynthia saw how willing Hal was to spend her money. She discouraged buying the old house so he agreed to drop it.

Cynthia realized they could spend some of her savings on a down payment and then income from the church would pay the mortgage and other expenses. Houses seemed to be too expensive so they started looking at condominiums. One of these was beautiful and new but still too high priced. It had only one bedroom, no extra space for Chantelle when she came.

They were well into autumn, and there was no jump in church attendance or income. Hal and Cynthia continued to argue about the reasons. She blamed him. They argued about Gretchen and the Church treasurer. Cynthia considered going back to work.

Hal and Cynthia did constant prayer for personal growth and insight into their own problems and situations. Often it had to do with childhood and relationships with parents. Cynthia began to have a lot of insight into her situation. In her family, her grandmother controlled everything by controlling Dad. Cynthia saw herself as her mother, who had no power. In the situation with Gretchen, she realized she saw Hal as her father and Gretchen as her paternal grandmother. Gretchen controlled Hal and had no consideration or respect for Cynthia. Hal allowed this to happen. He and Gretchen discussed things behind Cynthia's back. In the case of Chantelle's visits, Cynthia was fortunate if she found out when Chantelle was coming to visit. Hal accepted this and told Cynthia after the fact. Cynthia felt she deserved to be consulted, if Chantelle's visits were planned at random.

Sandra Hays, the church treasurer, was another Grandma. Hal had given Cynthia the job of coordinator of the Sunday school. Then she found Hal changing what she was doing; taking back the power he had given her. The reason was that Sandra's kids were in the Sunday school and she was going over Cynthia's head with matters regarding this. Hal, as Dad, had been unable to stand up to her and say, "Talk to Cynthia about it."

When she confronted Hal with this, he believed her. "Not only do I have Gretchen being Grandma, there is also Sandra Hays." She stopped there and he agreed with her, but all he could say was, "You are not all giving."

'I'm going to be even less giving." It appeared she had met with a dead end.

That evening they found a condo, which they liked and seemed to have all the things they wanted

Cynthia said. "It's too bad it isn't under better circumstances." All her insights and confrontations had interfered with what should have been a joyful event.

"It had to be done," thought Cynthia, referring to her confrontations with Hal.

Chapter 15: The Black Cloud

It was mid fall of 1988 that a black cloud descended upon the relationship of Cynthia Daniels and Hal Carter. It was no one's fault really. It had to do with the loss of innocence, the emergence of Truth, raising its ugly head as it does in all relationships. It just does so more or less painfully in some cases than in others depending on the degree of innocence with which one enters the relationship.

As soon as Cynthia saw Hal as Dad and accepted him as such, and it took her a while to accept, she lost her innocence. She stopped hearing those honey filled messages on the answering machine. She found he ignored her at classes where at one time he had gushed over her and flattered her in the presence of the students. She could believe she had changed or she could believe Dad was disapproving of her to get her to conform.

The first time Hal turned on the silent, Dad, disapproving treatment, Cynthia found it devastating, especially when Hal found it easy to replace her with another woman who could do some of her job in the church, but not as well. He gushed over and flattered Anne, fondling her in an embarrassing way, giving her back rubs. Anne was also well off and could drop a goodly sum into the collection plate. She responded to the flattery and fondling, giggling nervously.

At the same time, Hal and Cynthia had chosen a condo, which was beautiful, affordable for them but not in the best location. A mortgage representative from a financial institution who made Cynthia very nervous interviewed them. He asked both

Cynthia and Hal many questions about their financial situations. Finally he suggested that they put a large down payment on the condo, forty per cent, with small monthly payments.

Later, he called Cynthia when she was home alone and recommended that the condo be put in her name alone. He had obviously done some checking into Hal's financial history and wanted Cynthia's money protected should the marriage fail. He also suggested that a legal agreement be written up to protect Cynthia in the event of the sale of the condo or a divorce. When Cynthia asked herself if her uneasiness about buying a home with Hal was justified, a professional had just confirmed it.

Next Cynthia went to a lawyer who wrote up a legal contract, which was very restrictive. Hal received nothing if they were divorced or if the condo were sold.

When she approached Hal with the news of a legal document, he roared, "What are you trying to do? Leave me out altogether. Why are you leaving my name out of the title?" He went outside for a walk to cool down or to make Cynthia feel uneasy, she didn't know which.

Cynthia eased up on the contract, granting him one fifth of the proceeds after expenses, if the condo were sold. She thought it might be easier to live with him if she did this

Cynthia pondered all these things. Had she married a con artist? Was he really after the small amount of money that she had? Should she try to get out of the marriage now? What was she getting out of this marriage anyway? Was there anything worth working for? All of these ideas were running through her mind when she decided to take a weekend away to get clear about everything.

She booked into a motel in North Vancouver on a weekend when Chantelle was coming. While she was there she visited a friend and contemplated her life. One thing she thought about a lot was money. Since Hal couldn't make a living at the church maybe she could take on the role of breadwinner. Then he could mess around in the church and it wouldn't matter what he earned. She would be free from all the work she did at the church and she could detach from it. All she needed to do was to find a job.

On Sunday night when she returned home, Hal said, "I had such a wonderful weekend with Chantelle. " To herself she said, "*Well bully for you.*" Outwardly, she ignored the remark. She hoped the church had gone well without her too.

The following week she proceeded to look for work, answering ads in the newspaper and going for interviews. She focused on her life rather than on Hal's and the church.

The next weekend was Remembrance Day and Hal had offered to take Chantelle as Gretchen had planned a romantic weekend with a potential lover.

"She sounded guilty when she told me about it." Hal said.

"You sound sick," said Cynthia "like you're not over her."

The weekend proved to be all giving again for Cynthia. She gave her Divine Feminine Program on Saturday, a successful women's group which attracted a large group of women and which Hal was jealous of. Sunday was taken up with church and on Monday, they had to visit the in laws again. Cynthia was in tears and let her stress show in front of Chantelle, when she should have simply refused to do some of the stressful activities.

"I'm tired and I don't want to go to your folk's place today. This is the only time off I've had all week end " she cried.

"Poor Cynthia," said Hal, "What am I going to tell them if you don't go? You have to go. What will they think? You didn't go last time"

She relented and went. At least she didn't have to cook.

Tuesday morning brought with it a surprise. A carpet and drapery store in Surrey phoned to offer Cynthia a job. The only problem was the position was going to interfere with their move to the condo. However, she accepted. After the phone call, Hal congratulated her by hugging her and kissing her, the first time he had shown any affection in weeks.

Chapter 16: A Career to Remember

At the same time that Cynthia was job hunting and she and Hal were packing to move into the condo, other changes were taking place. Someone from the congregation saw a church building for rent in Surrey. It was actually a funeral chapel. The current location of the church was in a storefront. Of course it would be nicer to be in an actual church with extra rooms for classes and Sunday school but the rent was higher and Cynthia being thrifty felt it was an unwise move. The church was barely paying its bills where it was. Hal, jumped at the chance to be more in debt and the congregation not knowing the full circumstances voted for the move. So with the other changes, the church was moving too.

Cynthia started her new job at the drapery shop with high hopes. She went out on calls, but found that she was selling virtually nothing. She didn't know if it was something she was doing or if the store was at fault. Her aspirations of being a breadwinner in the family were not materializing. As time went on, she realized it was the Surrey market. Now she understood why the Franchise she investigated earlier had tried to force the Surrey store on her. Many people were selling draperies out of their houses and basements at cost, so it was impossible for a store to compete.

At the same time Hal finally became desperate enough for money to consider looking for an alternate income. When Cynthia discovered he hadn't paid their health care premiums for three months, she was livid. They had divided their living expenses in half and somehow he always managed to avoid paying his half.

She yelled at him, "You can pay for tap dancing lessons to a woman who makes four times what you do, for Chantelle who has everything, but you can't afford our health care premiums."

"I need to talk to you," he replied. "I have taken a job at a car dealership, as a salesman. Please pay our health care premiums this time and I promise to pay my share for next time."

"Okay." said Cynthia, "but I am not happy about it."

It must have sunk in because, not only did he take the job as a salesman for a car dealership as well as his job at the church, he also talked to Gretchen and had the dance lessons waived for the time being.

Moving to their new condo was not as exciting as it should have been as the dark cloud was still there. Hal worked hard unpacking and putting things away while Cynthia took calls from her job at the drapery store. In the pandemonium, they discovered the coffee alcove in the master bedroom.

Cynthia knew this could not be the career she longed for. Neither could she work in the church with Hal. He managed to sabotage everything she and others did to make it grow.

Cynthia knew she must focus on her own career. She went to a counselor who told her to make a list of all the things she wanted to experience in a profession. She did this She listed her strengths, experiences, talents. With this information in the forefront of her mind, she arrived at a customer's home one afternoon to measure the windows for blinds. The customer was not home.

Cynthia decided to give the customer ten minutes. While she waited, the idea came to her - an introduction service for people who are spiritually minded. She could sign them up, reprogram them to have a perfect relationship, include a copy of a little book she had written, provide workshops and counseling all for the price of a membership. Everything she wanted to do would be included. She envisioned interviewing them from a white desk, in a room with venetian blinds. She would call it Soul Mates. Forgetting all about the client she was waiting for she drove back to the store to tell Hal her idea. There would be a place for him in the service too, giving seminars and workshops on relationships. Her old dream of working with a spiritual man could be realized. The introduction service may even bring a few people to the church if Hal didn't drive them away.

Hal was supportive of the idea, so Cynthia quit her job at the drapery shop and began designing brochures and advertisements for her newly formed service. She had to apply for a license and started running it out of one of the rooms in the church. Immediately, people started joining and signing up for a low price. And it seemed that there were matches for many of them. Out of a small number of people came some suitable matches and some unsuitable but enough to work with. Cynthia had created a business for herself.

Chapter 17: The Church Cries Out

With Cynthia's attention on the newly formed Soul Mates, the church began to feel neglected. Without her power, there was a downward movement in the church's progress. People stopped coming. There were no new people. Hal felt the shift and began to panic about it. He had to get Cynthia's attention back. He was walking around with a tense expression on his face. He brought his feelings to her one day in early spring.

"There is a Church Consultant in Seattle, the husband of a successful minister there who, we might be able to get to come and look at our church, consult with us and help us to make it grow. Would you be in favor of us getting him to come?" He asked in his sweetest voice.

Cynthia pondered the proposal for a few seconds," But are you willing to listen to him, to try anything he might suggest even if you don't like it?"

"Yes I am," he said, self-assuredly, "More than anything, I want this church to work. I am willing to do anything it takes to make it a success," he vowed.

Cynthia wanted to know how much the consultant charged and where might the money come from.

The church had some savings, which had come from a tithe, ten per cent of the church's income, which Hal had wanted to use to start a theology school. He suggested they use the tithe money to pay the consultant. Since Cynthia knew their chances of starting a theology school were about nil, she agreed. Of course they would have to convince the board.

Cynthia's last words on the subject were, "If you promise you will try everything the consultant suggests and if that still doesn't work, you will give up the idea of a church and get a regular job, then I will support you and help you with this consultant idea." Hal agreed.

Hal telephoned the consultant whose name was Will Bentley and he made an appointment to meet with Hal and Cynthia at the Surrey Church one afternoon. He talked with both at length, especially Cynthia. Will asked her to tell him like it was. So she did.

She told him how Hal was a control freak, how he wouldn't delegate any jobs to anyone. If he did delegate, he would take the job back again. Cynthia told Will of Hal's coldness and unapproachable manner and lack of ability to appreciate all but a few members of the congregation. She wanted to tell him about the inappropriate behavior he had with a few women but she didn't.

Will considered everything and came up with a plan. He suggested that Cynthia be made the Volunteer Coordinator. She would set up committees to do the work in the church. There would be fund raising, grounds keeping, coffee and refreshments, book and tape sales. Hal was to do nothing but prepare sermons and hold the vision of the church. Will wished them good luck and headed back to Seattle. He would stay in touch. Basically he saw Hal as the problem. Keep him out of sight and let the church grow. That's how Cynthia saw it.

The congregation was called together. Persons were appointed to head the committees. Sandra Hays was angry that she wasn't the Volunteer Coordinator. Anne Wallace was appointed the Treasurer, a mistake to be sure. One woman was to be paid a small amount to clean the church, so Hal wouldn't do it.

Cynthia knew she had to keep up the system and remain enthusiastic if it were to continue running and stay in place. She constantly thanked volunteers during announcements in church and had volunteer meetings with thank you cakes and other things to maintain the interest of the people.

Someone came up with the idea of having a garage sale at the church, after the drapery store where Cynthia worked gave the church a lot of readymade vertical and venetian blinds in exchange for a tax receipt. One weekend the church was as busy as a flea market selling blinds and many other items. Cynthia saw the money taken in and helped to count it, but when Anne reported the cash, it was considerably less. Were she and Hal dipping their fingers into the till to fatten his pocket book a bit?

There was a second busy weekend when a wedding was held at the church. For two or three weeks Hal was able to stay out of things and let everyone do their job. For two or three weeks, the church began to grow. Hal let it happen. Then gradually, slowly the lack of control got to him. The annoyed look took over his face. He started complaining to Cynthia and then to other volunteers about how they were doing their jobs. Then he would say to them, "It's okay, I'll do it." As hard as Cynthia tried to make him leave the volunteers to do their jobs, he was very soon cleaning the toilets and making the coffee again. Within a period of six to eight weeks, everything was back to what it was. Cynthia spoke to Will Bentley, who said he could only call it as he saw it. Hal terminated the contract with Will but refused to give up the church.

Cynthia had her Soul Mates going pretty well, so she dropped her church activity except for the only successful program the church had going for it, "The Divine Feminine", although Hal kept encouraging her to cancel it.

With their relationship at an all-time low, it was now late spring, early summer and they rarely spoke to each other. Cynthia stopped going to church, as did many others. She made frequent trips to Vancouver to promote Soul Mates and to interview prospective clients. She signed up for a public speaking course and booked speaking engagements at metaphysical bookstores to promote Soul Mates. She also took a part time job at a tutoring school to supplement her income as unemployment had run out. The church was the farthest thing from her mind when an unexpected event occurred. The church building sold. What a perfect time to shut it down.

Chapter 18: Hal the Man

Although the time was perfect for the church to close, the time was not right for Hal to close it. He was drenched in confusion about what to do. He talked to the congregation about the church's problem being location, location, location and the solution was to move it to Coquitlam. The next day he found another car dealership job and gave the church away to a female minister, who was waiting in the wings for it. The day after that he quit the car dealership and took the church back. Cynthia remained calm and continued with her work. After switching plans several times, Hal started the Church up in Coquitlam in a hotel. Cynthia attended once in a while. She dreamed one night that the chairs were all facing backwards. Two or three weeks later, that's the way they were. Attendance was at an all-time low.

During their time at the condo, their relationship was up and down. They always related well as friends and could talk about anything together. It was here Hal brought home some pink flowers to plant around their home, as he had promised. In addition to that he put a climbing pink rose on one side of the deck and a pink rose bush on the other. Cynthia was moderately pleased that he had kept one of his promises. Simba loved the condo and the location. The condo was however in a construction site so nothing grew very well. Behind the condo was a little stream, but the water was full of slime and muck. Like the marriage, it was polluted.

Cynthia had plans for the fall. She had been accepted to do substitute teaching and had found a location in Vancouver to teach workshops and run Soul Mates. She was considering selling the condo and moving to Vancouver, possibly without Hal, as that is where she wanted to be. One day she told Hal about her plans. They had many arguments, where Hal shouted at Cynthia and she didn't mince any words back.

One day Hal suggested, "I'd like to have Anne teach some classes with us."

"She's not teaching anything from my location," snapped Cynthia." She can rent her own space. The truth is she doesn't have the guts or the ability. She's always hanging on your shirt tail."

"You're just jealous of her." shouted Hal "When are you going to do something about that horrible jealousy of yours?"

"She doesn't have anything for me to be jealous about."

Cynthia was not the jealous type but she remained suspicious of Hal's relationship with Anne Wallace. One evening when classes were being held at the church, Cynthia passed by one of the rooms used for Sunday school. The door was closed but ajar a few inches and she could hear giggling coming from within. She recognized the voice as Anne's and the other person she was sure was Hal. What were they doing in secret? She was tempted to barge in but feeling fearful of what she might interrupt, she continued on her way. Later she confronted him about it.

"What were you and Anne doing in the Sunday school room?"

"I was asking her if she wanted to be on the board." He lied.

"That was what all the giggling was about?"

He looked guilty like he'd been caught. "You are always fingering and massaging her. What do you think it looks like to other people especially her husband?"

"Okay, I'll stop, Hal agreed. After that Anne cut back on her donations to the church.

On another occasion, Anne was at the church to do some bookwork. Cynthia left them together. When she went back, unexpectedly, she noticed that Hal's zipper on his pants was open. What were he and Anne doing when she came back?

When he was angry with her, he treated her like she was a, child, who had been bad and he'd give her the silent treatment. Sometimes, he wouldn't speak to her for days. They didn't celebrate their first anniversary because he wasn't speaking to her and he was staying late at the church to work that night. Hal was unpredictable. Cynthia never knew who he was. Sometimes he was a loving husband and other times he was hateful. One example was at the end of June, his class, which consisted of Cynthia, Grace and Anne the treasurer, was planning to have a little graduation ceremony and a party. Hal and Cynthia had an argument just before the ceremony and he chose not to be speaking to her. She had her hair done, put up in an elegant style and wore a black and white semi-formal dress. During the ceremony, he ignored Cynthia and played up Anne and how wonderful she was and what a wonderful speaker she was and what a tremendous contribution she made to the church. Cynthia was crushed but refused to show it. Holding her head high, she caught his attention. Later, when they had semi made up, he told her he had seen her standing around with some of the women and had asked himself "Who is that beautiful woman?"

Another time they were giving a course on prosperity at the church. Cynthia had to miss a couple of the classes to go to Vancouver to give presentations at bookstores. Hal told the class he didn't know how he could continue teaching without Cynthia. He wanted to be with her so badly. How could he change so quickly, one moment adoring her, the next hating her for some reason?

At this time, Hal must have been doing some introspection. Cynthia believed that deep down he was not a bad man. He had always got what he wanted by manipulating and controlling people. What prevented him from being really bad was his sense of guilt. At the time the church moved to Coquitlam he became involved in a group called the Gurdjieff Foundation. They were followers of a Russian philosopher named George Gurdjieff and they taught the" Fourth Way" or the" Work" which included modesty, humility, self-control, and all the qualities Hal did not possess. Basically he knew he needed what these people taught. He knew he was arrogant, ego-centered and "know it all." At first, the group didn't want to let him in but eventually they started allowing him to come on a trial basis. There was one woman in the group he hated because she shattered his ego.

Back at the Church, rumors began to spread mainly from Grace about Hal and Ann, the treasurer. So early in July, Cynthia angrily and impulsively listed the condo with a real estate agent. When a terrific offer came in on it at the end of July, she was flabbergasted, surprised, jolted, frightened that her goals were taking form so quickly. She was at the tutoring school when the offer came in and she couldn't concentrate on what she was doing.

She and Hal had a long talk and decided to let the condo go and to stay together. They decided to move to Vancouver, where she would continue to run Soul Mates, teach workshops, substitute and Hal would commute to Coquitlam on Sundays. They had to split the proceeds from the condo as per the agreement with the lawyer. Hal received one fifth after expenses were taken out of his share. Cynthia received the balance, which she invested in T-bills. Hal gave some to his mother to repay an old debt and who knows how much to Gretchen, for dancing lessons in arrears. In any case, he soon went through his share.

That August they proceeded to look for a place to live in Vancouver and to pack again.

Chapter 19: Opportunities and Changes

August was house hunting and moving month, for Hal and Cynthia. She was not optimistic about moving, as she knew they would have to pay a lot more for a place as nice as they had in Coquitlam. Hal had no attachment to homes so he was ready to move on.

One day they planned to view a townhouse, when Cynthia received an answer to a resume she had submitted to a career college in Vancouver. The principal wanted to interview her for a teaching position. The trip to Vancouver turned out to be fruitful. The townhouse was smaller and older than their condo in Coquitlam but it was homey and nestled in some trees and shrubbery. It was on W.12 Ave, a busy street and was most unsuitable for Simba to go out. The rent was high but they didn't have condo fees to pay and felt they could handle it.

When Cynthia had her interview with the principal of the Horizon College, she felt most optimistic. The position was half time teaching English as a Second Language and Life skills to immigrant students. If she got the job, she could run Soul Mates and do her own workshops in her own time. Cynthia nearly died of excitement when the principal offered the job on the spot to begin in September. This would clash with moving and unpacking. Everything was working out perfectly according to her goals. Whatever Hal did with the Church, was up to him.

The move was traumatic for Cynthia. She hated leaving the little home she had tried to decorate as much as money would allow. Hal was optimistic about the new place.

"We'll paint it and fix it up," he said.

"What about Simba? We'll have to keep her on a rope like we did in New Westminster." lamented Cynthia. Finally they were packed and ready to go. Cynthia shed a couple of tears as she put Simba's carrier in the car.

For the first three weeks, Cynthia had to commute to Coquitlam until she had completed her job at the tutoring school. Then she began her job at the college, which she found she loved, both the work and the students, who were immigrant women mostly Spanish speaking. They were all very sweet ladies, eager to learn.

She strolled to work along the West Broadway area passing many old buildings imagining she was in London or New York. Walking to work was something she had always wanted to do. She interviewed clients for Soul Mates at home and for the time being didn't need an office. Hal drove to Coquitlam on Sundays for church.

During the summer, Cynthia was to take a walk along the beach at English Bay, where she had a vision of an introduction service in that area. In her vision, she had an office in that area with white venetian blinds. The same day a gypsy fortuneteller told her to hang on to her money, that she was in grave danger of losing it.

The month of September was heaven. The weather was perfect, the trees were vivid, and it was truly a break before the storm, which would come in October.

One quiet Saturday evening, the telephone rang, a call came which would change Cynthia's life for years to come. The woman on the other end of the line, in a shrill voice was enquiring about Soul Mates. Then she said she was Rachel Kaplan and that she had an introduction service for sale.

"What is the name of it?" asked Cynthia

"The Pink Rose."

Cynthia's heart leapt in her throat as "The Pink Rose" was one of the largest, most well known services in Vancouver.

"What are you asking for it?" asked Cynthia. The price was a lot but was within Cynthia's price range after selling the condominium.

"Why are you selling it?" was the next question.

"My husband has invented something that is going to make

us very rich," said Rachel." We want to retire to the States."

"Do you mind telling me what this invention is?" asked Cynthia.

"It is a devise to go on a toilet, to take away the smell," said Rachel.

"Maybe we can get together, this week to talk about it further," suggested Cynthia.

Cynthia set up an appointment for that week at The Pink Rose office for Hal and her to talk to Rachel and her husband. When Cynthia told Hal, he was delighted because he saw a place for himself in the business. Somehow in Cynthia's mind, a toilet invention didn't go well with a pink rose, but that did not dampen her enthusiasm.

Chapter 20: The Deal

Hal and Cynthia entered an interesting, but not posh, packaged office decorated in antiques. Rachel was a large well-dressed woman as was Rod the man she passed off as her husband. Later they admitted they weren't married in spite of their logo "the relationship people for the marriage minded." Together they painted a glorious picture of a lucrative, flourishing, fulfilling enterprise and acted as if they were interviewing Cynthia and Hal for the position of successors.

Their sales pitch was full of testimonials of how they had gone from rags to riches using their faith and hard work.

Rod said, "In 1986, the year of Expo, Rachel and I were down to our last few pennies. We had $3.61 in a piggy bank. That's all we had in the world. We sat on the couch, put our arms around each other and we cried. And we prayed and we cried and we prayed. We looked out the window and we saw the construction site for Expo. And it then hit us. Where were all those people going to stay for Expo? The hotels and motels would all be full. Why can't we start a billeting service, first listing rooms and suites in homes and then assigning travellers to these accommodations? We knocked on doors and recruited billets for people to stay. Things fell into place and over the summer made $267,000.96."

Rod and Rachel told story after story like this how they had made the "Pink Rose" grow from the previous owner in eighteen months. Hal and Rod hit it off particularly well comparing careers, which included car dealerships, and preaching in churches.

Hal asked, "This invention must be quite lucrative, if you want to sell the "Pink Rose?"

Cynthia flinched at the thought of a toilet attachment making them rich but she pushed the thought away listening only for what she wanted to hear which was all the money, fame and fulfillment she was going to have. For a moment she remembered the gypsy fortuneteller.

After talking with Rachel and Rod, Cynthia let her inflated ego tell her it was an opportunity from Heaven. Hal was even more ecstatic about it than she, the concept of them being the "the relationship people for the marriage minded" He would have given Rod and Rachel Cynthia's money that afternoon but she needed time to ponder the idea. The deadline for making the decision had become October 21st. Over the weeks that followed, Cynthia was torn between feelings of excitement and feelings of terror. Hal was no help. When she suggested they try to offer them less money for it, Hal was against it. He wanted Cynthia to be penniless.

He said, "If we don't pay them what they are asking they may not help us as much as they have promised." Hal was desperate. Church attendance was down to about twelve people. He was seriously ready to close it and had someone ready to take it over when he did.

Finally Cynthia made the decision to go ahead with the deal but it didn't rest well with her. She and Hal decided that he would give up the church and come to work with her at the Pink Rose as matchmaker as they did not want to keep Rachel's matchmaker.

Cynthia's lawyer suggested a precautionary clause be written into the contract. It stated that Rachel not be allowed to own or work at another introduction service in the lower mainland for a three year time frame. Rachel balked at this and Hal yelled at the lawyer, "Just put it through, damn it!" However, Cynthia listened to her lawyer and included the clause. But she was again disappointed in Hal's stance on the matter.

The whole fiasco took its toll on Cynthia. She relied on sleeping pills at night. It affected her work at the college during the day as she was so worried she would have to cut her hours or quit altogether. She did not mention anything to the principal at this point in time. She began having nosebleeds, a sure indication she was stressed.

Cynthia spoke to her lawyer, accountant and friends. All encouraged her to be careful but wished her luck. The one person, whose advice would have been most valuable, was not there for her. Her gut said "No! No! No!" God said, "I'm here, I'm here!" The truth is she wanted it so badly; she went to the bank on the twenty-first of October and withdrew the money. She gave up her job at the Horizon College, a job that she loved very much, because she didn't trust Hal with her business after what he had done to the church. She had to protect her investment.

When she had given everything away, her money, her job, her power, she received, in return, a key to a door ... a door to many surprises, and a key to hell.

Chapter 21: The First Day of Hell

October 22, 1989, was Cynthia's first day of her new business. Hal had actually gone in and spent a morning getting trained with Rachel ahead of time. Rachel must have turned the phones off, as there were no phone calls. Hal had taken Cynthia's car, Rachel had the only keys to the Pink Rose office and any hope Cynthia had of joining Hal and Rachel there for the afternoon. She sat trapped at the Horizon College completely stripped of her power, having to take a taxi, while Rachel and Hal munched away on a leisurely lunch. It was all symbolic of how she had given her power away.

The first day that The Pink Rose began for Cynthia and Hal was, about eighteen months after their marriage. Rachel was not there; she had left with Cynthia's money. Cynthia and Hal had the place to themselves. They decided to divide the work up between the two of them. Cynthia would handle the information calls and sell memberships. Hal would use his intuitive nature and do the matchmaking. They would share much of the work. The first day, in fact, the first week and the first month the phones rang constantly.. The phone calls were nothing more than "heat calls" as Hal called them. They were angry – no, not angry people - they were furious people. They were people with murder on their minds. Some made threats. "I'll see that you are closed down." Or, "I'm going to start litigation." Others wined and cried.

Complaints from angry clients took most of Cynthia and Hal's time and energy at first. They were people like Cynthia who had been sold a dream and paid a high price for nothing. The new business couple spent countless hours meeting people, interviewing them, calming them, comforting them, discussing them and trying to match them. One of the first things Hal and Cynthia did was to drop the logo "relationship people for the marriage minded." Cynthia found she could not sell. There was so much negativity around her that she was trapped in it.

Through all this unproductive work, there remained that old word that was constant in Hal and Cynthia's marriage. Money. They were not selling many memberships. That meant, bills could not be paid, rent at the office and at home, child support, etc. Cynthia's mood was not one for selling. She was floundering in insecurity, lack of confidence and fear. It had been easy selling memberships for Soul Mates. The fee was small and she believed in what she was selling. She did not believe in The Pink Rose for many reasons.

One of these reasons was that the client list she bought appeared to contain no assets only liabilities. Clients who might renew memberships after two years had actually been sold a lifetime membership. Many of Rachel's clients had a bad taste in their mouths. If they had not been successful in finding a partner in two years, they weren't anxious to sign up for two more years. Another difficulty that Cynthia faced was keen competition. The one person who could have supported Cynthia sat in his adjoining office, closing the door while he interviewed a client and treating Cynthia like she was the secretary rather than the owner of the business.

Month end was approaching. Cynthia sat down with the cheque book, her bills, the bank balance, her accounts receivable. Thank God for some small cheques which Rachel had charged some of her clients for monthly dues, another little surprise for everyone. Cynthia could pay everyone except herself, and she did have her last pay cheque from Horizon College. Gretchen, of course, would get her share.

Cynthia decided it was time to have a talk with herself. Here she was with a big overhead, the business not making much. It was her business and her money. The business couldn't support two people so if someone had to go it wouldn't be her. She was certain of that.

She wasn't quite ready to speak to Hal yet, when he talked to a client and closed the door to her office so she couldn`t hear what went on. When the client left, she blurted out. "I have to talk to you. For one thing I am sick and tired of being treated like the secretary in my own business." She handed him his pay cheque. "This business won't support two of us. If it is only going to support one of us, it is going to support me. It is my investment. You'll have to find another job."

Hal was getting ready to leave the office." We'll talk about this later."

"Please leave your key," she demanded.

He stared at her for a few moments. Then in his car salesman voice he said, "Well I hope you can handle this heat by yourself. Good luck paying all these overheads alone." He tossed the key on the desk and left.

Now Cynthia was alone in her expensive office with very little business, a large overhead, a pile of rubble for clients and her savings seriously depleted. She did the only thing she could do. She lay down on the floor and cried.

Chapter 22: Flying Solo

The floor, where Cynthia lay, was pretty uncomfortable. She wasn't sure how long she lay there. One thing that flashed through her mind while she lay there was Simba. She had left the poor little thing at the vet's that morning with a painful swelling on her anus. Was it a boil or something more serious like cancer? She had to get up if for no other reason than for Simba. She also hoped it wasn't going to be a huge bill.

The other idea that came to her mind was one of the scriptures, of Paul where he is contemplating one of his afflictions. As Cynthia considered her helplessness the words of Paul came to mind. "My power is perfect in weakness." She felt the power of her creator fill her and had a sense that she could get a hold of her hopeless situation and turn it around. Then she rose from the floor and took a sheet of paper to make a list of things she could do on a physical level to make things easier for herself.

Since Hal was no longer going to be there she decided to get rid of his office and cut down on some expense. She went to see the property manager about giving up the one office. To her delight, Dorothy had another single, front office available slightly larger, with white venetian blinds, facing the street. The venetian blinds were as her vision so while she was at it, she asked for a white desk too.

The phone system would be simpler too for one office and less expensive. Dorothy was totally supportive and when Cynthia told her what had happened, regarding Hal, she said, "Women are always better business people than men anyway." Cynthia went back to her own office relieved that Rachel's vibes would soon be gone.

She next reviewed some advertising that was expensive but not bringing much in terms of interested people. She cancelled it and left herself open to something less expensive and more productive.

While she was busy with all of these changes, the phones started to ring. To her surprise the calls were not complaints, but information calls. People wanted to know about the service, making appointments and wanting to join. She had several appointments for the next few days.

Before she knew it, the day was coming to a close. She had not heard from Hal all day nor had she thought about him. Before she left, she wondered if he had been looking for a job or if he was thinking of starting another church. She didn't want to face him and the foul mood that he might be in.

Before she left the office she called the vets who told her that Simba had only an abscess and could be picked up. Cynthia was relieved the dear little thing would be all right.

Hal was already home and dressed in casual clothes. He'd been looking through the want ads and was in a quiet, pensive mood.

He said, "Hi, How are you?"

Cynthia answered, "Hi," in a tired voice, in return and there were no arguments. Simba was wearing a cone to prevent her from licking her wound and Cynthia was relieved that the terrible task was done and she had survived her first day of flying solo.

Chapter 23: The Hope for Peace

Cynthia approached her second day alone at the Pink Rose by cutting more expenses. She decided to give up her parking space downtown at the hotel and to walk to work, about one and one half miles. It was also good for her health and weight.

Her greatest worry was that Hal would want to start another church. Glenda Moore, who was very supportive of him in his Vancouver church, was still in town and looking for work. Cynthia feared Hal would link up with her and offer her a position. Hal, she knew had to have a woman to do the church thing with him.

Cynthia decided to phone Glenda to warn her and also to find out if Hal had approached her about a church. She told Glenda about what had happened at the Pink Rose.

"He may get an idea about starting another church and ask you to work with him." Cynthia told Glenda. "I just wanted to warn you. Stay away from him. I have had enough of churches with him, to know it doesn't work."

Glenda replied, "You don't have to warn me. I know better now. I lost a lot of money to him. He's a typical dry alcoholic. You have had that experience with him. And now you are finished enabling him."

Glenda's words struck home with Cynthia and she felt that she had done the right thing in firing Hal even if she felt sorry for him. She also felt sure Glenda would not support Hal in another church. Cynthia was surprised to learn that Hal had taken money from Glenda.

"Are you looking for a job? You could try the tutoring school. And also the Horizon Collage." Cynthia encouraged Glenda, hoping she wouldn't be tempted to try to work for Hal at a church.

At the office, over the next few days, Cynthia was able to sell a few memberships and took in enough money to pay the December bills. She also made a few matches and felt she was really taking charge and taking things into her own hands. One match however, she was to live to regret, as it came back to haunt her in a few months. She matched a woman of about sixty years with a bartender of about fifty. The woman had requested a younger man and also someone Italian, which he was. However, the woman was insulted that the man was not of high enough social class and she was very angry.

The woman shrieked at Cynthia, "He was only a bartender. You introduced me to a bartender. I wonder what his income is. I want a refund and if I don't get one, I will start litigation."

At home, Hal had good news, "I found a job. A Toyota dealer has hired me to lease cars, some in large fleets to rental companies. "Let's celebrate and go out to dinner!"

At the table, he ordered a large steak.

Cynthia then said something she regretted.

"I was enabling you. When I fired you, I freed you up to get a good job.

"You're not taking the credit for this. I got this job myself," he snapped. The dinner ended on a bad note. Cynthia threatened to walk home from the restaurant.

Cynthia was grateful for the time being, at least that there was no talk of church. Her prayers that they could have a peaceful marriage where they could each work and where he could pay his share of the bills were answered. He could possibly help satisfy his need to give workshops at the Pink Rose in the New Year.

Chapter 24: The Good

With Hal at a paying job, Cynthia could breathe a little easier. She didn't have to worry about the church or the business not bringing in enough to pay his half of the bills. He could even afford to take her out for dinner once in a while.

Gretchen remarried and released her grip on Hal a little, as she had someone else to manipulate and control. She also had a new lease on Hal as she wanted her new husband to adopt Chantelle but at the same time she expected Hal to keep paying the child support money. Hal refused to give up custody but did agree to let the child take the surname of her new spouse. Cynthia managed to stay out of the camaraderie, but Hal began to see Gretchen more for what she was, a carnivore. Since Hal had given in on the surname, he had more leeway on the visitation times. Cynthia felt relieved for a time away from Gretchen's clutches.

After moving to Vancouver, a larger distance from Abbottsford, they were not obliged to visit Hal's family as often as before. This was another great relief for Cynthia but a source of guilt for Hal, which he could blame on Cynthia.

Hal was often nice and considerate toward Cynthia. He usually arose before her and brought her coffee in bed, something she appreciated very much. Once on Mother's Day, he gave her a card with cats, which was addressed from Simba. Cynthia showed only mild appreciation. Hal was disappointed that she didn't jump up and down with emotion, as Gretchen would have done. However he did learn from the situation that Cynthia was not Gretchen and didn't react with strong emotion. Cynthia had hopes the marriage would grow and survive.

Cynthia was amazed at how Hal was tuned in to her. One day she took a diuretic pill only to discover that it didn't work at all. She didn't urinate once, but instead Hal was up all night going to the bathroom. And she had not told him she had taken it. Another time she had taken a sleeping pill, again not told him, spent a sleepless night. Again Hal had found he could not stay awake. She wasn't sure she liked this closeness.

This closeness was demonstrated when Cynthia lost Simba. Cynthia decided that when Simba died she would not replace her, at least not right away. Instead, she would wait until she felt like she really wanted another cat. About three months after Simba's death, one evening she felt very strongly that she wanted another cat. She didn't decide when, she just said to herself, "Yes I do want another cat." She didn't tell Hal or anyone else. The next day she had a cat.

She was home, when Hal phoned from the office and said, "I've made a decision. I'm going to get you a cat. I picked one out at the SPCA. She is black with a little bit of brown and has a face like Simba."

"That's very strange, because I decided yesterday that I wanted another cat." said Cynthia

He picked the little cat up at the SPCA that afternoon and brought her home. She lay on their bed that night.

"I think I'd like to call her Nikki," said Cynthia

"Do you love her?" asked Hal.

"Not yet, but I will." said Cynthia

After Simba died, Cynthia was so grief stricken that they decided to move again to get away from the pain.

There were close moments like this that Cynthia cherished, when Hal could be loving. Sometimes they took short weekend trips to the States or Victoria where they had tender moments together.

Although no longer employed at the Pink Rose, Hal was supportive of any problems Cynthia had. One match Cynthia made resulted in a lawsuit. He came to court and backed her up. They ran classes and workshops from the seminar room, which allowed him to do teaching, which he loved.

A common spirituality gave them something to talk and pray about. Cynthia hoped that their marriage would work. She loved Hal but felt that sometimes she was in denial about it working. She had a feeling that one day it would end.

Chapter 25: The Bad

Without the church to embarrass Cynthia, there were still other events and issues to bring shame to her and to what she considered her good name. There were phone calls from creditors on behalf of the church, which had not paid its final utility bill and other debts. Cynthia finally said, "I don't want any such calls coming to my home. I don't care what happens to the church's unpaid bills; just make sure they don't come to my attention."

There were also personal creditors. Hal owed a debt he shared with Gretchen's father (now deceased) from many years back. Cynthia doubted if a debt such as this had any validity but Hal in order to keep in Gretchen's good books set about to pay it. Such a matter threw a thorn in the side of a struggling marriage.

There were a lot of devious personal calls coming to Hal at home. Some were old clients, all female, whom he had counseled at one time or other and now wanted help. Hal explained he was such an indispensable counselor that they had fallen in love with him. It happens only when counselors are very good, he added.

After he became involved with the Gurdjieff group, one such client appeared who needed help very badly. She was a nurse and was very emotional. He had to sneak out to see her telling Cynthia he was going grocery shopping. If Cynthia questioned him, he would say, "It's just your horrible jealousy again."

Of course their largest problem, which resulted in their first and last fight and in Cynthia planning eleven separations, was Gretchen. Gretchen would call Hal every Monday morning after a weekend of observations and directions for how he should be handling Chantelle or not handling Chantelle. Cynthia would recognize his car salesman voice and his negative attitude toward her.

It took Cynthia a while to figure out what had happened. Then she realized there was the Monday morning call, then came Hal being negative and critical toward her and then some new plans for handling Chantelle's visits. Finally, Cynthia approached him on the subject.

"Hal, I've figured it out. Why you are negative toward me on Mondays. It is after you talk to Gretchen. She must really lay it on you. Then you pass it on to me. Then we fight."

An example of this occurred one Monday when she had come home from the Horizon College where there was a Curry Restaurant. She commented on having a headache after smelling curry all afternoon. Hal accused her of being negative.

Hal thought about it for a while and agreed, but only for a time. After having to agree that he had been talking to Gretchen, he began to lie and say, "No, I wasn't talking to Gretchen."

Cynthia couldn't win when Gretchen had Hal on her side. Whenever Cynthia suggested the truth that Gretchen was manipulative or coercive, Hal would fly into a rage and deny it. Once he threw a plate of food across the room. The truth made him so angry. He would also use the silent treatment and stay out for all day and late at night. He would not speak for several days. This was his way of controlling the situation. Cynthia would go into a depression and make plans to leave him. Then they would make up and the separation would be delayed.

Other things they fought about (besides Chantelle and his parents) whom he accused Cynthia of hating were his other three children. She hit him right back with, "You hate your kids and you hate your parents," which he knew was the truth. He wanted to blame the strained relationships onto her.

Sometimes they fought about sex. He would complain he wasn't getting enough. "Its okay, honey. It isn't Sunday. You don't have to have sex today."

She would explain how they would rarely have a chance to have sex as he worked late and read Gurdjieff books late into the night. The truth was she dreaded having sex. She felt dirty, tainted after having sex with him. She tried to save his feelings by not telling the truth but he didn't have any regard for hers at all. "I guess you just don't like sex." If he had added "with me," it would have been the truth.

They did escape some of Gretchen's nagging after Chantelle took the new surname and Hal could see Gretchen more for what she was.

Then the brick hit the ashes. Gretchen and her new hubby split up. Everyone especially Hal's parents were moaning "poor Chantelle". No one felt sorry for the poor brow beaten husband. All of a sudden Hal was jumping through hoops to be Chantelle's dad and Gretchen's husband again. Cynthia didn't mince any words, "Why don't you move into Gretchen's doghouse and they could whistle when they had a morsel for you and needed you to babysit."

Cynthia began to feel her marriage no longer had a prayer now that the trump card was back in Gretchen's hand again.

Chapter 26: The Ugly

It was May, 1991, three years since Hal and Cynthia had married and eighteen months since the birth of the introduction service. The marriage was hanging by a thread depending, which way Gretchen decided to pull it. The latest thing she'd done since the desolation of her marriage was to buy a farm in the interior of British Columbia. How this would affect Hal's child custody rights, Cynthia didn't know.

Victoria Day weekend was approaching and Hal suggested they go to the island for a little get away. He looked after reservations for the ferry and hotels at various stops along the way. Cynthia had hopes the little trip would provide a pleasant relief from the busy work schedule at the Pink Rose.

The first place they stopped after disembarking from the ferry was Lady Smith where they had dinner and stayed overnight. The next morning Cynthia brought up the subject of Chantelle.

"She'll be moving at the end of the school year won't she?" queried Cynthia.

"Yes." said Hal, "She'll be going before that. She'll be going after next weekend."

"I didn't know that," said Cynthia. "Then I won't be seeing her again before she leaves."

"Well, she'll be coming next weekend to stay," said Hal.

"What, she's coming to stay next weekend?" gasped Cynthia. "Nobody told me that. Are you planning things with Gretchen behind my back again?"

"I told you about it. That she was coming for the whole

weekend, before she moves to the interior," he shouted. "You just forgot."

"You told me nothing. Are you trying to tell me I have Alzheimer's? You are lying because you don't have the guts to face me." '

He looked beaten. "You and Gretchen have me cornered so I don't know what to do. I should let you talk to her".

"That's the best idea yet," said Cynthia. "I thought we agreed, you are to discuss it with me when Chantelle is coming to stay. Now here you are planning things behind my back again. Why can't you stand up to that woman? What kind of a wimp are you?" Cynthia had never used such strong words with him before.

The argument ended there. It was not finished.

"I want to go home," demanded Cynthia.

"Don't go home," pleaded Hal.

They ended up finishing the long weekend, but Cynthia had a bitter taste in her mouth. She wanted to complete the discussion they had on the trip.

When they got home, she made a point of setting a time to talk to Hal. As soon as she brought up the matter of him making plans for Chantelle to come without including her in the plans, Hal was ready for her. He was on the defensive to put it mildly. To say he was wild with rage would be more specific. It was not open for discussion at all.

He said, "You are not going to tell me what to do with my little daughter!"

Cynthia said, "I am not trying to tell you what to do with her. I just want to be included in the plans since it is my house. I don't want plans made behind my back."

He began shouting and waving his arms.

She said, "Now you are acting like Jesus."

He said, "God bless his Holy Name."

The arm waving continued until he slapped her across the face as hard as he could. She felt shocked and made for the phone so she could call the police, but had second thoughts. Feeling stunned, she knew she would not tolerate a man hitting her.

"I'm leaving you," she shouted.

She got her coat and purse together not knowing where she was going, but he started blocking the doors so she couldn't get out. Finally she was successful in leaving and she drove to the office where she sat down to think. *I can't live with a man who hits me. It's over.* After a couple of hours, she returned to the apartment feeling numb, beaten and knowing that her decision was made for her.

She slept badly on the couch and awoke in the morning feeling hung over, tired and headachy. Hal had got up early and left for work. Cynthia knew the first thing she needed to do was to find a place to live temporarily and then permanently.

She called a friend who did house sitting.

"You're leaving Hal?" asked Josey in a not surprised voice. "I don't know of a place right now, but Glenda Moore does." Glenda had spent her college years doing housework for her board. "I'll get her to give you a call."

In a few minutes, Glenda called back. "You've decided to leave Hal," said Glenda, also not surprised. "You can stay with me. I am staying in a basement suite in a house belonging to an old lady. You'll have to sleep on the couch."

"It will be just fine," said Cynthia. "I just need a place until I can find an apartment, probably until the first of June. I really appreciate it, Glenda."

"We'll have lots of fun," said Glenda, who was a bouncy, bubbly person.

Cynthia was anywhere but having fun. She felt devastated.

She dressed and prepared to go to the office. Once there, she busied herself with appointments and phone calls. She also slipped out a few times to look at apartments.

It turned out to be a busy productive day. Cynthia signed up a male client at 6:p.m.and didn't finish until 8:00. She then went home to pack a few things to move to Glenda's place. Hal was lying on the couch.

"Are you leaving?" he asked.

She said yes and then ignored him. She packed enough things to last a few days, told him where she was going and gave him a phone number for emergencies.

She arrived at Glenda's at around 9:00 p.m. with a take-out hamburger, the only food she'd had all day.

Chapter 27: Single Again, or "1991"

Cynthia stayed with Glenda Moore for a few days until she found a small apartment in the west end and took Nikki with her. Hal stayed in the larger one until the lease was up in the fall. Chantelle had not come for that drastic weekend. Gretchen and Hal must have had it out, but it was too late to save the marriage. Hal and Cynthia divided their belongings amicably so they only needed to buy a few new things each.

Cynthia found separating from even a terrible marriage difficult, uncoupling, she called it. She felt stretched, pulled apart. Each time she did it, it became more difficult and more difficult as she grew older. She knew she would never do it again; she would never marry again and never separate again. No more coupling, no more uncoupling.

The office flourished as it always did when she and Hal quarreled. She claimed her power back when they were on the outs and her work showed it. The week she left him was very productive. She told no one about the separation, only a few friends.

On the surface, she was in control making things work. Underneath she was wounded, needing to heal. One emotion she felt more strongly than disappointment and hurt was anger. She was furious with Hal and with Gretchen. She would wake up in the night, so angry she couldn't get back to sleep. She hoped that time would be the healer.

One evening about three weeks after she moved, Hal invited Cynthia out for dinner to a nice restaurant. He came all dressed up and she wondered what his motive was. It didn't take long for her to find out what it was. As they sat at the table he cut to the chase, "Would you be interested in having a sexual relationship with me?"

He caught her off guard but didn't surprise her. She answered him immediately.

"NO, NO, NO! That is the one thing I am most thankful for in our separation. I don't have to have sex with you!"

"Okay" was all he said.

The remainder of the meal was in silence and then he drove her home. She was thankful he had asked and not tried to seduce her. Sex was probably one of the things he missed most in the separation.

She grieved for so many things. Not so much for him but for the idea of a relationship. The part of her that related was gone- ripped out of her and she grieved for loss of that part.

During the first year of separation he asked her twice about moving back with him. There was no mention of confronting any of the issues in the marriage. Just let's get back together. She refused. After one year had passed, she got the forms ready so they could file for divorce. She was very clear that she wanted to end it. Hal agreed.

Chapter 28: The Secret Letter

Sometime during the second year of her separation, 1992, after the divorce became final, Cynthia's loneliness became extreme. Of course the devil, in the form of Hal, was there to court her. He began to take her to barbecues, harbor cruises sponsored by his work, movies and dinners. Of course, she and Hal always communicated well. He told her he enjoyed talking to her because she always made him think. They began seeing each other nearly every day and talking on the phone every day. Cynthia was ashamed of her weakness but her loneliness allowed her to be swept in.

Hal began pressuring her to have sex with him. She put him off as long as she could. They planned a weekend in Harrison Hot Springs and she was afraid she would relent, which she did. He kept saying their relationship had picked up right where it had left off. Every time he said that she would say "But it isn't going to work because we haven't dealt with any of the issues yet. This little affair is just temporary."

This is what it was, an affair. She still found sex unsatisfactory, like she was being bullied into it. He thought everything was solved.

Then it was time for Gretchen to emerge, to make her entrance again. She had moved to the interior and Hal was in the habit of going there once a month to visit Chantelle. Cynthia could feel his edginess as the monthly visit came closer. First he asked Cynthia if she would like to go with him and stay in a motel but she refused. Then she found him being argumentative so that he would have an excuse to go by himself and stay at Gretchen's with whatever sleeping arrangements. She could tell by his negativity that he had been talking to Gretchen again. He began accusing Cynthia of not accepting his family.

Cynthia said, "I have no need to have any of these people in my life. That includes Gretchen, Chantelle, your mother, your brother, I haven't missed any of them one iota over the past eighteen months. They don't add one droplet of anything to my life. I can understand why you want to have a relationship with Chantelle but don't expect me to share you with Gretchen."

"I see you still have a problem with my family," said Hal.

"No, you still have a problem with your family," snapped Cynthia.

Hal was silent.

For the next couple of days, he was distant and cool, back in his Gretchen mode. Cynthia knew this would come, knew there was no hope of them reconciling. The next evening he brought her home from somewhere and instead of coming in he handed her a letter at the door.

She was shocked. It was so unlike him. Had she done something? She tore the letter open. The contents couldn't have surprised her more.

Dear Cynthia

I want to tell you about something that happened a long time ago when I was still drinking. I used to have blackouts and would wake up and not know where I was. One day after such a blackout I found myself engaged in sexual behavior with my eldest daughter, Tracey, not intercourse but mutual handling and fondling. I was so ashamed; I apologized to her and went to the priest for confession. He gave me penance to do. Jane, my first wife, knew about it but pretended she didn't.

Recently Jane wrote letters to everybody in my family, my parents, my brothers and Gretchen telling them about this. She told them Dad had done this to some kids when he had them bobbing for candy in his pockets. After he got her letter, he took so many sleeping pills he went to sleep for a week. Jane said my brothers should be watched, as it may be a family trait. She also told Gretchen she should keep Chantelle away from me.

Gretchen reciprocated by sending Chantelle down to stay the

91

weekend with me.

I feel I owe so much to Gretchen for that.

I was always worried that you would find out. Please destroy this letter.

- - Hal

Cynthia was in shock. There was some reason why Tracey was so angry with Hal. And Cynthia always felt a niggling concern for Chantelle when Hal was alone with her. But why had he written her the letter? Why now? What message was in it for her? She called him and told him she wasn't surprised and that she needed some time to work through the letter. She would call him in a few days.

Chapter 29: Lung Cancer

Over the next few days the emotions Cynthia experienced were devastating. How could she have misjudged someone so much especially someone she trusted enough to marry? She felt pain for Tracey who had carried the abuse with her throughout her life. No wonder she had always been chilly toward Hal. She could have brought charges against him.

Cynthia had always felt niggling suspicions about Hal and his daughters. Now to discover they were true. What other behaviors of his, she suspected were also true. When she suspected he was feeling up Ann Wallace at the church was he actually doing it?

What kind of woman and mother was Gretchen, would flaunt her young daughter in front of a known pedophile even if he was her father and she loved him. Were Gretchen and Hal playing some kind of control game? I'll taunt you with my daughter if you prove you can leave her alone. Or perhaps it was worse. Perhaps he was abusing Chantelle with Gretchen's blessing.

The situation explained Cynthia's own sexual feelings toward Hal. She always felt like a child being bullied into sex by her father, although she didn't really know what that felt like, since she'd never had that experience. Bullying children was perhaps the only way he could relate sexually.

Cynthia needed some research on pedophiles. She phoned some social service agencies and found out - no pedophiles never change. If they abuse one daughter, they'll abuse another. The people she spoke to all wanted Cynthia to report Hal and Gretchen but she didn't.

Cynthia examined Hal's past behavior. The women he was always attracted to were a certain type. They were childlike, little girls. He had trouble relating to mature women. There was a woman in the Gurdjieff group he couldn't stand because she was mature and assertive. Another woman in his classes was girlish and he liked her. It all fell into place. Cynthia didn't know how she fit. When she and Hal got along, she must be childlike and when they fought she was behaving as a mature woman.

Finally, why did this letter come to her? Why did he tell her about this abuse at this time? She could only come up with one reason. He was desperate. He was playing his ace card. Cynthia was refusing to have him in her life with Gretchen in his life. If she accepted Gretchen, she accepted his debt to Gretchen. He was manipulating her into letting him keep Gretchen. "No. I'm sorry, Hal. I can't do it."

She called him in a few days as she said she would.

"I don't want to see you again," she said. "I think your letter was an attempt to manipulate me."

"So you think I am being manipulative?"

"Yes."

"Can I call you?" he asked.

"No, I don't see much point in it." she said.

The conversation ended. Over the next few months, she again went through being hurt, being uncoupled, being self-effaced for having misjudged him so badly. She worked hard. As well as working at the office, she did substitute teaching. She bought a small condo near the office. Her life prospered except for being lonely.

One day about eighteen months after the letter, she taught at a school and experienced a dead battery in her car near a Canadian Tire store. The store was next door to where Hal worked. Contrary to her good judgment she popped in to say hello. She was told Hal was at home. After stopping at the office she called him from home.

He answered right away.

"I am off sick," he said.

"What's wrong?" she asked. Hal was never sick.

"I had surgery," he hesitated. "Lung cancer"

Cynthia was shocked. "Oh, Hal, you'll have to quit

94

smoking!"

"I have quit smoking. I quit while I was in the hospital. I was on the patch. I had to have two patches a day."

"How long were you in the hospital?" asked Cynthia.

"Five weeks. When I got out, I was bored so I went back to work for a few hours a day for something to do."

"How bad was the cancer?' Asked Cynthia. "Do they think they got it all?"

"They removed about three quarters of the lung but the tumor was only the size of quarter."

"Did any of your kids come to visit you while you were in there?" asked Cynthia.

"My folks came but not any of my kids," said Hal. Cynthia was surprised that not even his precious Chantelle had come. She felt pity and empathy for him and said, "Heaven forbid if you ever get it back, let me know and I will help you in any way I can."

After that he recovered quite well and invited her to the odd movie, Bard on the Beach, the Shakespearean play, or dinner at the Normandy the restaurant on 12th Ave near where they used to live. She went out of pity or loneliness. There was no sex, but in spite of all he had done, she knew she would always love him.

As time went on he did a lot of coughing and the doctors x-rayed his lungs periodically claiming them to be cancer free. They diagnosed him with COP Disease, Chronic Obstructive Pneumonic Disease, once known as Emphysema and Chronic Bronchitis. He began to worsen having colds coughs and flu, quite frequently. One evening after a supper out, he sat down on the loveseat, ashen in colour, and coughed incessantly. It was at that instant; Cynthia knew she was losing him, although she knew not when. She discovered he was cancelling many events including father's day and Chantelle's school play. One Friday night, he called her and asked her to come over, as he was sick. She tried to help him by getting medicine, from the drug store, when he seemed to have flu. For the most part she tried to get on with the rest of her own life while keeping her commitment to help him should the worst come to pass.

Chapter 30: 1995

It was another uneventful Saturday afternoon. The telephone rang breaking the silence. Cynthia answered it and a male voice at the other end asked, "Rawlene?"

"No, you must have the wrong number." she replied. The voice sounded familiar. The reply came in a croaky tone, but at the same time it was a deep resonant tone.

"Sorry," it said.

Cynthia was about to hang up when the familiarity of the voice struck home.

"Is that you Hal?" she asked.

"Yes. Who is this?" The croakiness was very pronounced.

"It's Cynthia."

"I've got you on automatic dial and must have pushed you by mistake," he explained.

"What's wrong with your voice? Do you have a cold?" she asked.

"It's those inhalers," he said. "They make my throat dry."

"Do they help, at least?" she asked.

"They did at first, but now not very much. How are you?" he asked.

"I'm fine. Who were you calling?" she asked knowing it was none of her business.

"Oh, just this woman called Rawlene," he replied.

The conversation soon ended with a usual, "Talk to you soon."

After hanging up Cynthia realized that Hal must have a date with Rawlene. That was his mode of operation, to phone Saturday afternoon to confirm a date Saturday night. And Rawlene, what a name! It sounded like a new age title which many of the granola girls acquired along with their sudden transformation to spirituality. That was about Hal's speed. She was, probably from his Sufi group. Cynthia put the matter out of her mind and continued on with her boring Saturday afternoon.

The following Wednesday was the extraordinary meeting of the Strata for her building. A very narrow majority was voting the management company out so the council decided to go out for a drink after the meeting to celebrate. It was eleven thirty when Cynthia returned to her apartment. There were calls on her answering machine when she glanced at it. One of them was from Hal asking her to call him back. Knowing he never went to bed early, she called him back.

He picked up the phone immediately and in his "dentures out' voice, asked where she had been. She explained about the meeting, the victory and the celebration after and then let him get around to why he had called. It turned out he wanted to invite her to an outdoor Shakespearean Theatre, which they attended in previous years. She accepted before she had a chance to think about it and added, "We'll have to take along some cushions for the hard seats."

Before he had a chance to consider it he added, "They have soft ones this year." Then he hesitated, "At least I heard they do."

And then true to form, he agreed to phone on Saturday to confirm. "Maybe we can go for a picnic before the play."

After she hung up the phone, she decided this going out on dates with him must end. It was not consistent with her goal to get on with the rest of her life. Actually she only went out with him two or three times a year and there was no physical contact but it had to stop. She knew he had lied to her about the chairs. He had obviously been there, probably the week before with Rawlene. She considered saying to him, "You don't have to lie. We aren't married any more."

In the two days that followed, she considered telling him she wasn't feeling well and bowing out on the date. She wanted to start anew but somehow she was bonded to him with pity and an unconditional type of love.

That Friday was the last day of school and she came home completely exhausted from a difficult assignment that had lasted for ten days. She went to bed early and got up with what felt like a head cold. Deciding to use that as her reason for not going out with Hal, she lay in bed resting before she had to go out for a doctor's appointment.

Around 9:30, the phone jolted her with its sharp ring. Hal must be calling early. She stumbled to the phone and a woman's voice asked for Cynthia Daniels.

"This is the charge nurse at Vancouver General Hospital," she continued. "I'm calling from the cardiac ward. Mr. Carter was admitted here early this morning. He asked me to call you and let you know." It was like a knife wound, a familiar pain that she had felt before.

"How is he?' she faltered.

"We've just drained some fluid from his heart," said the woman, careful not to give out too much information.

"Thank you for calling me," said Cynthia. "Tell him I will come and see him a little later."

A sick hopeless feeling had come over her. She had felt it before when her sister had become terminally ill and died. Her father, as well. It was a familiar feeling and she knew what it meant. The feeling stayed with her as she went to see her doctor about a wart on her finger, a spot on her nose and some anti-depressant pills. All seemed so trivial compared to what she faced at the Vancouver General Hospital. She had suspected that Hal was going to die but she didn't know it would come so soon. As she drove to the hospital she tried to imagine it was not something serious but as much as she tried, the sick hopeless feeling remained.

Chapter 31: The Diagnosis

Parking was a problem at the General Hospital. Cynthia drove into a parkade, not wanting to be towed, and walked to the entrance to the hospital. Once inside there was no information desk with a live human being but instead a telephone, which you called to get the location of a patient. The female voice at the other end found Hal in emergency in the cardiac department. It instructed Cynthia to get on an elevator and to follow a yellow line that would take her to the right location. She followed the endless yellow arrow with a heavy heart. One part of her dreaded what lay ahead while another part needed to know the truth. After being certain she was lost and stopping to ask more than one staff if she was indeed on the right path, she eventually ended up on the other side of the hospital in emergency. This however was not her final destination as she was then directed on to another nursing station surrounded by curtained off beds

When she inquired as to Hal's location the nurse hesitated. "He's very sick," she said. "Are you family?"

"I'm his ex-wife," said Cynthia, knowing this hesitation was a bad sign.

A second nurse spoke up and said, "It's okay, he wants to see her."

The nurse led Cynthia to one of the curtained off beds, where she saw Hal lying with an oxygen mask on his face. At one glance she took in some circular metal objects on his chest, some reddish stain and a heart monitor on his finger. Her eyes went to his face which was drawn and pale. She gently kissed him on the forehead.

"Hi!" he said, "I asked them to call you and let you know I am in here."

"How are you?" she asked.

"I'm a little better than I was at four a.m. when I came in here. They thought I was having a heart attack. I was so sick for hours at home. I didn't know what to do. I left work on Thursday noon because I felt so bad."

"Why didn't you call me? I could have come to help you and could have driven you here. Did you drive yourself?"

"I didn't want to bother you," he said in his independent way. "Yes, I drove. It is only a few blocks and I managed to get the car here somehow. It's parked out on the street."

Just then, a young male doctor who entered via the curtains interrupted them.

"Are you feeling any better?" he asked.

"Not much," answered Hal

"We drained quite a lot of fluid from your heart and we're going to do the same with your lungs. That should get you breathing a little better." The young man then left as quickly as he entered.

Just then Hal was overtaken with a coughing fit, which interrupted their conversation. Once recovered, he said, "I don't know long I will be in here. I'm anxious to get back to work."

"Don't worry about work. Your health is more important. Anyway it is a long weekend. Monday is a holiday and most people are taking it off." Cynthia said this knowing that work was the least of his worries, as if he'd be going back to work at all.

Hal was again seized with a coughing fit. He sat up straight in bed and leaned forward coughing and wiping his nose and mouth. As he finished she got up enough courage to venture the question.

"What do they think it is?"

Looking at the tissue, he said quietly, "It's the cancer."

The words struck her hard. She had expected emphysema, or chronic lung disease or perhaps fluid buildup where the piece of lung had been removed, but not cancer! How could she have been so stupid? She had not considered the possibility, but of course now it all added up.

She stammered "But I thought they said your tests and xrays were all clear." She clung to that belief for a moment, denying what she was hearing and yet knowing in her heart all the time that it was true.

"I guess they missed it," he added, adjusting the oxygen mask. "The young guy, he found it. I've known for a while." Then he added, "I had those lumps in my neck a while back." Cynthia didn't know about them.

"Then they think it is the cancer back? Oh God, no."

He looked angry and waved his hand for her to retreat and then added, "It's okay. I'm not afraid of it anymore."

Tears welled in her eyes but he still did not look at her. She took his hand and said, "Let's pray." They started with the Lord's Prayer, then the Yogananda prayer. She was almost through the Twenty-third Psalm, when the nurse barged in through the curtains. After the nurse left, Cynthia stopped denying the news and some of the tension left the room.

"I should have taken you to the hospital that night you called me. I'm sorry," she added.

"That pain was back again, like I had that night. That's what it was, the cancer."

"Is there anything you want me to do?" she asked. "Is there anyone you want me to call and let them know you are here."

He shook his head and then reconsidered. "I was supposed to go to my folks' place tomorrow. Could you please call them and tell them I can't come? You could also call Tim?"

Chapter 32: The Proposal

Cancer is a dark, vicious intruder who steals into lives and bodies moving slowly and soundlessly, a masked and hooded stranger whose goal is death. It had stolen into Hal's and as it did other bodies disguised as many less dangerous names, emphysema, chronic lung disease, flu, bronchitis, colds, completely deceiving its victims and the medical profession. Then, as it makes its final attack, claiming complete victory, it destroys any hope that its deception may have provided. Cynthia knew she had been tricked, deceived and betrayed. All the faith she had put in medical reports and diagnosis were nothing but red herrings in cancer's deadly plan.

She managed to drive home in spite of the tears that poured from her eyes. She kept thinking of what a sad life Hal had lived and now for it to end in the worst possible way.

She found the telephone number of her former in laws with whom she had no contact over the past four years. On the first try, no one answered, although she knew they rarely went out. Mrs. Carter answered on the second try. She was not sure what to call them but decided on Mr. and Mrs. Carter.

"Hello, Mrs. Carter, This is Cynthia. I am calling to let you know that Hal is in the hospital. He is really sick. They think his cancer has returned."

"Oh, thank you for calling us," she said. "We've been trying to phone him for a few days."

Hal's mother appeared grateful for her call. She indicated they would not be able to come to see him until Art and Trish returned from their trip to Alberta. Mrs. Carter said she would call Chantelle and Janine, the latter who had moved to Alberta. There was also Tracey. The conversation ended with Cynthia saying, "I'll go back and see him later in the day and will call you back. I'll also let Tim know."

Tim's phone number was easy to get from directory assistance and she left a message on the answering machine. Then she sat down to gather her thoughts. The tears continued, crying being something she had not been able to do for a long time.

Cynthia had the need to call someone to tell the news. She decided to call Margaret, a friend who was a minister. Margaret answered right away and Cynthia poured out her story. Margaret invited Cynthia to a movie and to go to dinner after.

Cynthia made one more phone call to her church to ask for prayer for Hal. Then she realized she had better hurry if she were to go to the hospital before the movie.

This time Hal was resting again but had a simpler oxygen mask on. They had drained his lungs again, but he wasn't sure that it had helped. He said that Tim had been in and must have received Cynthia's message.

Hal then asked her, "Are you coming tomorrow?"

"Of course" she replied.

"What time?" he asked.

"I'm supposed to go to New Westminster if the weather is good. It will probably be around twelve. Your folks want to come and see you but they have no way of getting here as Art and Trish are in Alberta."

"That's good. I don't want to see them very badly."

Hal seemed tired and not wanting to talk so Cynthia decided to leave him for now. She said she would check his car one more time.

When she arrived home she just had time to call Mrs. Carter to tell her she had seen him.

"I talked to him about dying," Mrs. C. said. "He said he isn't afraid to die."

"All we can do is pray for him," said Cynthia. "I'll call you tomorrow after I've seen him."

The next morning she entered the curtained off area where he sat in bed with the oxygen mask on his face.

"I'm worse today," he said. He paused and then continued.

"Gretchen was here this morning. She has gone to my apartment to clean it up. I left it in such a mess when I came to the hospital."

Cynthia gasped. How did that bitch manage to get there so soon? It was so like her to show up to make sure nothing happened that she could not control. Did she drive all the way from the interior this morning or was she in Vancouver all along? Cynthia didn't say anything out loud but groaned inside.

He paused again. "I've got the cancer back. It's everywhere." He made a hand gesture to signify his whole body. "They say I've got a week, or maybe up to a month. I may be able to go home for a while."

The words struck her again as they did the first time. "So soon?"

"I'm so sorry." she said the tears again filling her eyes.

"Its okay," he said. "I want to die."

"Are you sure?" she asked.

He nodded, coughing.

"Well, I don't think you are going to miss anything," she added through her tears.

"I've got to get my affairs in order. I have a will somewhere. Gretchen is the executor," he said.

"Oh no," said Cynthia. "I thought you picked Art for executor."

Hal immediately replied, "You and I were not on very good terms and Tim didn't show signs of straightening out." He paused. "She's a good woman."

"I didn't like what she did to you or our marriage," Cynthia said.

He ignored her comment. "In my will, I have requested an Anglican funeral and I want to be cremated. Will you look after that?"

"Of course," she agreed. "Do you have any money for a burial?"

"I don't know. Maybe if I sell everything off. The funeral will have to be cheap. And I don't want a tea. Just a small funeral with family and a few friends."

She had hoped to bow out once she had notified all his relatives but now she was getting more involved.

He paused again. "I never had any relationships after you because I always loved you," he said.

104

"I didn't either, "said Cynthia.

He was leading up to something. "I was wondering if we could get married. Then you could have my Canada Pension. I would like to give you that."

Cynthia couldn't believe what she was hearing. "Oh it's not necessary," she said. "I know your heart may be in the right place."

"It's something I really want to do," he added. "You don't have to sleep with me."

She touched his hand and smiled. "Oh no," she said.

"It would mean you would get about four or five hundred dollars a month. If am not married, no one gets it. We'll have to find out how long you have to be married before the widow can collect the survivor's benefit. Can you phone and find out on Tuesday?"

Cynthia was still not convinced. She had the feeling this might just be another of Hal's pipe dreams that would ultimate end up in a disaster. She was sure she did not want to inherit any of his debts, as it seemed his financial affairs had not improved since they parted.

"Okay, I'll phone around. There may be a lot of pit falls. It may be difficult to get a marriage license on short notice or we may need copies of our divorce decrees that might not be readily available and we may both have to go to the license bureau." She pointed out.

"Could you please find out?" asked Hal. "I really want to do this."

Cynthia was unsure about doing it but she felt this was not just a whim but probably something he had been considering for a long time.

'Okay, I will think about it," she agreed. "And I will phone around on Tuesday morning."

"Please do. It would mean so much to me," said Hal.

"I'll also talk to Joe at the church about the funeral." she promised.

"There is something I want you to do. If we go through with this, I want you to tell everyone in your family. Tell them that it is your idea. I don't want anyone claiming I coerced you on your deathbed," said Cynthia.

"Okay, I can do that," he agreed. "I want you to consider the whole idea. We don't have much time."

The conversation then switched topics. He told her the doctors were going to do a surgery on him that afternoon. They were going to insert a tube from his lungs to his stomach to drain the fluid that kept accumulating in the lungs. The purpose was to keep him breathing a little easier, to make him a little more comfortable until the end.

Cynthia was still tearful resigning herself to the truth. "I think you'll like it over there on the other side," she said.

"I don't know," he said.

The nurse came in at that point and began adjusting and manipulating objects as nurses do.

Hal said to the nurse, "Can I have some morphine? I'm a bit shook up."

The nurse agreed. The doctor must have left orders he could have all the drugs he wanted for the pain. She returned with a large hypodermic needle and said, "This may sting."

After the injection, he lay back in bed and said, "I don't know what time the surgery will be but there is a chance I won't make it, if I don't just remember that I love you."

Cynthia asked, "Is there anything else I can do?"

"Just be happy," he replied.

He looked about ready to sleep so she asked about his car again and he replied that Tim was going to take it back to the dealership the next day. Before she left she promised to get the necessary information on Tuesday and she would call later to see how the surgery went. She left the hospital feeling overwhelmed.

Chapter 33: Time to Ponder

Cynthia woke up Monday morning to a phone call from her old archenemy, Gretchen. Gretchen was at home in the interior and was confused about Hal's life expectancy. She thought he had said he would be in the hospital somewhere from a week to a month. Cynthia straightened her out, "No from what he told me, he has from a week anywhere up to a month to live."

Gretchen didn't believe her. "Could you please find out for sure?" asked the old manipulator. Of course the old accommodator said yes and agreed to make a trip to the hospital to confirm what she already knew.

When she got there, Hal had been moved to a semiprivate room.

"Did you get the marriage license?" he asked.

"No, that's tomorrow," she said. Then she told him why she had come. He confirmed that the doctors had given him from a week up to a month to live.

Cynthia drove home and called Gretchen back and conveyed the news. Gretchen started crying. Cynthia wondered how sincere her tears were.

Gretchen said, "I'll have to go to Penticton to tell my mother. She was always fond of Hal. Also I'll have to bring Chantelle down maybe Friday." Then she hung up to shed some more tears.

Hal's parents were expected that afternoon and Cynthia not wanting to see them decided to stay away from the hospital. This gave him time to talk to them about the marriage idea and her time to ponder Hal's proposal.

Many questions came to her mind. Was he trying to manipulate her? Was this one final attempt to get her back? Probably. Was the Canada Pension an attempt to lure her back? What about his debts? If she married him, was she responsible for his debts? The answer was no. She found a lawyer open on the holiday that answered her question. She would not be responsible for his debts.

Another question was what if she married him and he had a spontaneous remission? What would she do? Make the best of it or get another divorce. She decided a spontaneous remission was unlikely and she would face that possibility if it happened.

All other offices where she needed information were closed until the next day so she'd have to wait to talk to Canada Pension and the Marriage License place. She called a few close friends to see what they thought she should do and also saw a psychic for a reading. All came up with a resounding YES, do it.

In the late afternoon she returned to the hospital one more time to visit Hal. Tim was there and was in tears. Hal looked overwhelmed. "Mom and Dad were here and Art and Trish." he looked disgusted. "I've had my moment."

Cynthia said, "They love you."

Hal clearly didn't want to talk, as she hoped he would. Finally, he said to Tim and Cynthia, "I love you both very much but I need to sleep. I'll see you, tomorrow." Cynthia left reluctantly.

When she got home she made the other call she needed to make. She phoned Joe the Anglican priest at her church to see if he would look after the funeral. He assured her he would be around the whole month of July.

Chapter 34: The Decision

On the Monday, Cynthia had lots of time to contemplate. Margaret had promised to call after ten and when she did, Cynthia poured out her feelings. She spoke of her anger over the past four years, with Hal and with Gretchen, how she had not been able to put her anger aside and get on with her life. She spoke of how this marriage may allow her to complete that part of her, to forgive and move on. She spoke of how Hal seemed to need to give back something of what he had taken from her, of how he wanted to die married and at peace.

On Tuesday morning Cynthia received a call from the hospital to bring back Hal's wallet, as Gretchen needed his I.D. to do the work as executrix. Cynthia made her phone calls and found out yes it was a simple task to get a marriage license, one person could get one and no divorce certificates were necessary. The Canada Pension Plan was a bit iffier. A couple needed to be married or living common law for one year to qualify for the survivor's benefit. Would they consider her case, with two marriages to the same person? The lady at the Canada Pension office thought so, but she urged Cynthia to apply. Cynthia went to the hospital with the wallet and she supposed her decision. Hal gave her one hundred dollars for the marriage license.

Janine and Gretchen were both there. Cynthia hadn't seen either of them for four for five years They both had aged. Hal made a comment about Janine being his little princess and Cynthia being his "special angel". Cynthia flinched, as both were terms used by sex offenders for their prey. Just as Cynthia was leaving, a tearful Tracey, his eldest daughter, whom he had abused, was coming in.

Cynthia didn't recognize her, but later Trish mentioned that Hal and Tracey had an emotional forgiving time together.

Nevertheless, Cynthia bought the marriage license and they planned the wedding for Wednesday morning early while Margaret was on her way to the golf course. Tuesday evening when Cynthia went out for something to eat, Hal left a message on her machine that he was looking forward to tomorrow.

In the morning, she dressed in a nice dress, her wedding shoes, put her wedding band in her purse and drove to the hospital. Hal was dressed in a morning jacket. The nurses had him shaved and looking chipper. He told Cynthia and Margaret how he had woken up three times in the night thinking he was cooking at an Italian wedding. He was very upset that he was losing it.

Margaret got on with the wedding ceremony she had written and affirmed with Hal that he wanted to go through with it.

"I love this brat," he said as if Cynthia didn't deserve it.

"And she loves you too," said Margaret. She then proceeded with the vows.

In as much as you Cynthia and Hal have come again to the Holy State of Matrimony, I accept and celebrate that you have returned to this state because of deep soul recognition of your eternal unconditional love for one another. I also recognize and declare that this is a completion for both of you in our physical life.

This sacred and precious ceremony now frees both your soul Cynthia and your soul Hal at a deep level to move on to a great love and peace to what is divinely each one's to do.

This having been said and felt before God, each other and these witnesses I ask that you Hal, do you take Cynthia to be your Wedded Wife?

Hal said, "I do."

I ask you Cynthia, 'Do you take Hal to be your Wedded Husband?'

Cynthia said, "I do"...

By the power vested in me by the Province of British Columbia, I now pronounce you Husband and Wife.

Margaret then said a brief prayer.

The nurse and a patient in the next bed then signed the register and Margaret hurried off for her golf game. The same nurse who thought it all very exciting to have a wedding in the hospital, brought out confetti and wine glasses and ginger ale. Cynthia's emotions were a blank. Hal was elated. He said, "You're going to be a widow."

On the evening of the wedding, Gretchen came over to plan the funeral. A man who was recommended by Cynthia's priest as being inexpensive met with them. Hal was very certain that he wanted to be cremated, so the expense of a casket and grave could be eliminated. Gretchen played the old martyr and said she would have to take out a bank loan to pay for it until the Canada Pension money came through. Cynthia felt very uneasy about this.

Chapter 35: The Last Days

Cynthia didn't feel married. She felt many emotions, mainly confusion. One night, the Friday night, she decided to stay overnight with Hal and sleep in the opposite bed where he had had a roommate earlier. Early in the evening, as a cool breeze came in the window, he was feeling nostalgic about his childhood in Manitoba. As the night progressed he began losing it more and more. He began shouting at the nurses and at Cynthia. He said, "There are 2000 pounds of worms out in the yard and I have to go and pay for them."

He started accusing Cynthia of marrying him for his money and talking about some type of conspiracy that she was instigating "My own wife." he shouted. He ranted and raved and spoke in tongues, which he had previously told Cynthia he could do and she had never believed him. The nurses kept giving him more and more sedatives to calm him down as he was trying to escape from the hospital.

At 5:00 am Cynthia decided she'd had enough and left the hospital. As the sun was coming up she walked up West 12th Avenue toward the car to go home. She felt cold both inwardly and outwardly. She knew she would not be spending any more nights at the hospital. Once home she got into her warm bed and slept late into the day. She told Margaret what had happened and Margaret's reply was always wise, "Cynthia, this is about freedom."

The nurses agreed to put an orderly on at night to restrain Hal so that family members wouldn't have to put up with abuse. Cynthia had hoped to opt out of Hal's dying days but being married to him she gave her word to his family that she would help sit by his bedside. Consequently, her's was the evening shift.

The next day Cynthia spoke to Hal's brother Art, who told her Hal was asking for her that he wanted to talk to her. Was he aware of how abusive he had been the night before? What did he want to talk to her about?

Janine, Hal's second daughter and Gretchen were both staying at Hal's apartment and were in and out of the hospital throughout the last days. Cynthia learned from Janine that Hal had divided his life insurance policy, originally intended for Chantelle alone, among his four children. Here Cynthia was his wife and knew nothing of his will or his business and Gretchen had control of it all. Later it proved to be an advantage for Cynthia.

One day when he was more lucid, Hal told Cynthia he had three pieces of jewelry for her, a cat broach, a pink stone necklace and two silver chains. They were somewhere in his apartment and he would ask Gretchen to find them for Cynthia. Cynthia asked Gretchen herself and also asked Janine to look for them since she was also staying there.

Cynthia went to the hospital on the Sunday morning, to meet up with Hal's parents and brothers. His mother said that Hal had been asking for Cynthia and that he wanted to talk to her alone. Cynthia entered the room to find Hal very confused. He seemed to be looking for his glasses He started to say something but didn't finish. A man from the Gurdjieff group came in. Cynthia believed she should have insisted on privacy with Hal as she never seemed to have a chance to talk to him and she wanted to before he died.

Gretchen started cleaning out his apartment and giving away his belongings before he actually died. Cynthia was to get a television set. She felt sick talking about it, especially when he was still thinking he might be able to go home for a little while.

As the days passed, Hal's condition worsened. He needed more and more oxygen. He spoke to them less and less. The Gurdjieff people were in and out playing taped music and trying to read to him from the "Tibetan Book of the Dead' so he would let go of this life and move on. The woman, who was always phoning Hal when they were married, and Cynthia was suspicious of, was there. She told Cynthia how Hal was still in love with Cynthia and how she had tried to phone Cynthia to tell her. Chantelle was in and out with her mother. Hal acted as if he couldn't care less if she were there or not. Everyone was waiting for him to die.

Cynthia went to the hospital each day at around 7:00 p.m. after the others had all left. She felt lonely, as he was no longer very lucid. He was worried about things like his dentures. On the Tuesday evening he had another violent episode but it was more directed at the nurses than at Cynthia. He tried to find his clothes and said to Cynthia, "See if you can get us out of here." Cynthia left at 11:00 p.m. when the male nurse came on duty.

On Wednesday morning, Cynthia woke up with a feeling that today may be the day. She phoned the hospital and the nurse said, "You had better come." She dressed and went over about 8:00 a.m. She found Hal breathing heavily, refusing his breakfast. Gurdjieff people were playing their toneless music and reading to him. Cynthia stopped his doctor in the hall and asked him the question, "How much longer do you think it will be?"

"Probably today or tomorrow," he replied.

Cynthia called Gretchen and told her to come. When Gretchen arrived, she called Hal's mother, also Tim and Tracey. They all came except Tracey. Hal wanted to talk to Gretchen alone. Cynthia said, "I think she has everything looked after."

"Yes, but she won't tell me anything," he said and then slipped back into delirium. Did he doubt the trust he put in her? Cynthia assured Hal he would soon be seeing his Grandma Carter whom he loved very much and a dog he had as a kid.

Cynthia was in a daze, wandering around the hospital with Gretchen, Chantelle and all of Hal's family, all waiting for Hal to stop breathing. She lost track of time in her confusion. At one point she got on the elevator with Chantelle, who said, "They are all full of guilt, except for me and my mom."

Cynthia nearly threw up. Chantelle and her mother had the most guilt of all. She had to get out of there. She had to go home for a while. She would tell them she would come back at seven like she did every day. After all she had been there since eight in the morning. She couldn't take it any longer. And she had had no time to talk to him alone.

Once at home she did some laundry to busy herself for a while. At five thirty, the phone rang. It was Janine. She said "Gretchen says you better come back. He's going."

"Okay," said Cynthia. "I just had to get out of there for a

114

while."

"Oh, oh," said Janine. "Gretchen says he's gone."

"Okay," said Cynthia. "I'll be right back."

Once at the hospital, Cynthia saw that the nurses had unhooked everything and everyone was viewing his still body. She was sorry she was not there when he passed but she didn't want to be there with his whole family. She touched his cold forehead and said, "You're free."

Cynthia noticed that no one not even his precious Chantelle was shedding a tear. No one offered her a hug and she didn't feel like hugging them. She felt numb. They all seemed relieved it was over.

Chapter 36: The Funeral and the Burial

At the hospital Gretchen prompted Cynthia to call the church to book it for the funeral and the tea afterward, even though Hal did not want a tea. It was booked for the following Saturday. Gretchen called the man at the funeral parlor to arrange for the cremation. The nurse removed Hal's wedding band and gave it to Cynthia, as were Hal's wishes. Cynthia would keep it always.

Everyone began to scatter. Cynthia walked with Janine to the car. A skinny black and white cat jumped up and followed them. Janine said, "Maybe it is Dad" Then she pulled the jewelry from her purse that she found at Hal's apartment that was intended for Cynthia, a cat broach, pink stone necklace and two chains.

Janine began to talk about the Canada Pension. Apparently, Hal had told her that he wanted Cynthia to have it, as he owed it to her. He wanted her to have it instead of Gretchen as he had given Gretchen Chantelle, as if you could compare money with a life.

"I'm glad he's gone," said Janine. Everyone, it seemed, was glad he was gone. Except Cynthia, who had wanted to have one last talk with him. Unfinished business. One last chance to right his wrongs.

Cynthia slept poorly. She did have one dream that he was in a river, riding the rapids toward the east. Over the next few days following Hal's death Cynthia felt an emptiness she could not explain. It *was* the same emotion she was sure she would feel if she had had a real marriage, instead of a week long one. She felt real grief, real pain and real loss. She couldn't cry however, she had done that already.

The funeral was very serene, Joe the priest didn't know Hal, but he gave comfort to the family. Even the evangelical members were impressed. The music was appropriate. A Gurdjieff man, whom Hal admired, gave a short eulogy. Cynthia felt Hal would have been happy with the funeral.

She had asked Hal what he wanted them to do with his ashes and he said he wanted them sprinkled at a local garden at the waterfall. One morning Cynthia had a visitor. It was the mortician dropping off the ashes in a white cardboard box. Cynthia took the box he handed her and placed it on the television set. Cynthia was aware that, Hal, the man who had caused so much grief in her life had been reduced to a small box of ashes on her television set.

One Sunday morning, early, Tim and Cynthia went out to the garden to sprinkle the ashes around the waterfall. She read from Yogananda while he mixed the white ashes with the brown soil.

Soon all the family, Gretchen, Chantelle and everyone returned home and back to their lives. Cynthia was alone with her mourning. She filled out her forms to apply for the Canada Pension survivor's benefit. Her first payment came in about a month.

Chapter 37: The Gift

In about six weeks, during the month of September, Cynthia received a surprise phone call from Gretchen. She knew it wasn't a friendly phone call; Gretchen didn't want to be her friend. It was something more.

"Chantelle has been grieving so much for her dad," she started out saying. Then she cut to the chase.

"It seemed Hal had a pension with his employer, the proceeds of which were to go to the widow." She went on to say, "However, Hal had named Chantelle the beneficiary in his will. And so I need you to sign it over to her."

She went on to say, "I can't get my hands on any of her life insurance money as she is a minor and I need money to raise her. The two hundred dollars a month I get from CPP, as an orphan's benefit isn't enough. You'll have to get in touch with Hal's boss to sign over the pension and as soon as possible. Also an agent from London Life will be contacting you".

"I'd like to see the will," said Cynthia. "I am, after all, the widow."

Cynthia said she would phone Hal's boss but didn't promise to sign over anything without knowing more about it.

When Cynthia called Hal's boss, he said, "Yes, there is a locked in pension that you could put into an RRSP or roll over into another type of pension, but it cannot be taken out until the beneficiary is 65 years of age." He did not mention Chantelle, the will or signing it over to her. Cynthia had mixed feelings about this. Was this pension meant for her, Cynthia? She asked for a copy of the will but Gretchen ignored her request and instead sent a nasty letter threatening to annul the marriage and to see Cynthia in court.

Was this pension meant for her? At first, she felt guilty like she was taking candy from a babe when she thought of keeping it. As time went on, she began to feel more and more that Hal meant her to have it.

It was Christmas time when she finally signed the documents and the insurance company paid her out. She couldn't believe it was happening. The insurance company had written to her asking her why she hadn't signed it. The steps taken for this to happen were long and nerve wracking and she revealed them to Margaret, her friend the minister and mentor.

"It was a repeat of my old emotions about taking something away from my sister. When I became clear that Hal was not here to push my buttons about Chantelle being an emulation of my sister, I was ready to let go of any guilt about accepting the pension."

"Isn't it wonderful that you were able to see that, Cynthia?" said Margaret.

"I hired one lawyer who was so much like Hal and was completely useless. He allowed Gretchen to win him over to her side and tried to talk me into signing the pension over to Chantelle. That's how persuasive Gretchen is. I let that lawyer go and hired another one who was on my side. He told me I was the only one who could annul my marriage. She was threatening to annul my marriage."

"Imagine," said Margaret.

"The new lawyer also told me the will was null and void since it was written before the wedding. A marriage nullifies a will. Gretchen would have found this out if she sought legal counsel, as she threatened to do. I don't know if such a will even existed." Cynthia paused. "I didn't want to lose my Canada Pension, Margaret, as I suspected Gretchen would report me for marrying Hal just to get his pension. So I decided to come completely clean with CPP and wrote to them telling them of my two marriages to Hal, the second being a reconciliation. So far I have not had a reply from them."

"And you won't," added Margaret.

"I did receive a letter from London Life, the insurance Company, wondering why I had not signed the paper to receive the payout. I telephoned them back. They told me I was the true beneficiary. When I asked, they told me Gretchen had informed that I had married Hal for his Canada Pension survivor's benefit, but they had no reason not to pay me. That was when I finally signed the paper to receive the payout and asked to have it deposited in my RRSP. It is just another wonderful gift from Hal," said Cynthia.

"And he meant you to have it," assured Margaret. "Have you had any contact from Gretchen?"

"No, none at all", said, Cynthia, "She probably gave it up when she realized the pension was locked in and she couldn't use it. You see Chantelle was an emulation of my younger sister, who I was taught not to take anything away from. When I became clear that she was not my sister and that I was entitled to the pension, then it came to me. I've had so much growth from this whole process and am so grateful for the additional gift of money."

Epilogue: The Pink Rose.

In the summer of 1996, Cynthia took a drive to Coquitlam to the townhouse where she and Hal had lived from 1989 until 1991. She drove in the complex, following the route she took when she lived there. Many emotions crept up on her. She felt sadness and comfort as she parked the car in her old spot. She exited the car and walked around to her old home. She went carefully around the building. The fence was still the same. There it was! It raised its lovely head above the fence. It was the climbing rose that Hal had planted for her when they first moved in. He had wanted to plant pink flowers for her all around the condo. It was about a foot high when they moved out but now exceeded the height of the fence. Tears filled her eyes. Love once sown never dies. Cynthia realized that she had forgiven Hal for his shortcomings and his problems and that he could not be different from what he was. She had expected him to be different and had forgiven, not forgotten the past.

Love Was My Business: Memoirs of a Matchmaker

by

Sylvia D. London

Table of Contents

Chapter 1   In the Beginning

When people asked me, usually with stars in their eyes, how I got into the business, I always said, "I took a temporary leave of my sanity." Intended as a joke, the statement saved me from explaining the real, painful story, without actually lying about it.

It began in late 1988. A few months earlier, I had married the man of my dreams - tall, thin, spiritual and principled or so I thought. The second half of my dream, which was to share a spiritual ministry with that man, had also come true. There was just one problem; none of it was going the way I had expected. The man turned out to be manipulative, insecure, and abusive with countless financial, emotional and family problems. The church, which we shared, was a farce. As I tried to make it work for him, he succeeded in sabotaging all my efforts as well as his own or so it seemed from my naïve perspective at that time.

I decided to detach myself from the church and its problems and to focus on my own life. I desperately took a job in decorating which was my previous occupation. I believed that the marriage part of my dream could be saved.

The decorating job, like most acts of desperation, turned out to be pretty much of a disaster. Keen competition from people working out of their homes and selling at cost, made it financially not lucrative. In other words, I wasn't doing any business. It was also emotionally unsatisfying. The truth was my heart wasn't in it. My obsession about saving souls and helping them to live a fairy tale life still haunted me.

Upon the advice of a career counsellor, I proceeded to do some personal work. I made a list of my strengths, my experience, my talents, and those rewards I wanted to reap in a job. With this information at the forefront of my thoughts, I arrived at a customer's home one afternoon to measure her windows for blinds. As sometimes happens in sales, I was stood up by the customer. Deciding to give her ten minutes I waited in my car pondering my true purpose in life.

It was then the idea came to me. Of course, an introduction service for spiritually minded people! I saw myself signing them up, reprogramming them to have a perfect relationship, include a copy of a little book I had written about love and then matching them. All would be included in the cost of a membership. Everything I wanted to do was included. I envisioned interviewing them from a white desk, in a room with venetian blinds, selling my ideas and ultimately making their lives complete bliss by finding the right partner for them. My husband could also participate by helping to give workshops on relationships. My old two-dream would be realized. Dashing off to the store to tell him, I forgot all about my customer.

Little did I know that hundreds of others had come up with this idea before me. I didn't bother to research the business I was to discover that countless agencies had started up in the previous years and had subsequently closed again. In retrospect, it must have been my innocence that helped me succeed like the Fool in the Tarot deck who jumps off a cliff, taking an enormous risk and succeeds because he lacks the vision to fail.

This was in 1988. Since that time, on line dating services came about and are the way to go in the 2000's. Personal matchmakers have become a thing of the past. There are advantages and disadvantages to both. On line dating services are quick as there are no lengthy forms to fill out or interviews. They are also relatively inexpensive compared to a matchmaking system. However, the advantages of a manual match are many. The matchmaker knows his clients and works with them on a personal level. My story will reveal how I came to know my clients and to be able to match them more accurately based on their life situations, preferences and personalities.

I proceeded to design brochures, drafting my ideas,

applying for licensing and eventually advertising for clients. "If you build it, they will come" my own field of dreams. Charging a small fee at first I began. Clients started phoning and joining. I was in the introduction business!

Over the six years that followed, my life took a journey, a terrifying difficult journey that had I known what it would be like, I would have avoided at all costs. Nothing about the business turned out the way I expected. Financial and other rewards were few. An up hill roller coaster ride to hell, the business brought me to a place I would never reached through a thousand years of steady employment. That place was emotional maturity, the journey of a young girl into a woman - The Priestess in the Tarot deck.

Chapter 2   The Con

One Saturday evening, the phone rang. A woman at the other end of the line was enquiring about Soul Mates, my introduction service. She started asking questions as if she were a potential client. Then she told me she had an introduction service for sale. When I asked her the name of her service, she told me it was "Renaissance," which I knew to be a large and successful service in Vancouver. When I asked her how much she wanted for it, it was an amount I had.

Then I asked her why she was selling it and she told me that her husband had invented something and they were about to become rich from the invention. The invention was something to go on a toilet to take away the smell. It didn't sound very exciting compared with matching up people for relationships but I continued with the conversation.

She invited me to come to her office to discuss it further. I was interested, so I made an appointment with her for the following Thursday. When I told my husband, he was delighted as he immediately saw a place for himself in the business.

Her name was Sandi and she had the man, she passed off as her husband, with her. I wondered how people who advertised as "relationship people for the marriage minded" could themselves not make a commitment. They told us countless stories about their successes in the business. One such story was about how they were down to their last dollar and were desperate for money. They sat down on the couch and cried and prayed and cried and prayed. They looked out the window and saw the construction site for Expo 86. Then they came up with a plan. They would find billets for people looking for accommodation for Expo and rent them rooms. Over the course of a few weeks, they had made a huge amount of money. They told us many tales about how they had turned Renaissance around and made it into a lucrative business.

We were convinced. I really wanted to buy it. My husband could hardly wait. I should have done some more checking, but I could taste success. So I took the money out of my investments and bought it.

From the very first, I knew it was a mistake. The first few days were hell. The clients I purchased were all dissatisfied people who felt they had been swindled. The phones rang constantly with complaints. I grappled with insecurity and found I couldn't sell. People, who had been told they had bought a two-year membership, had poor service and were not willing to re-join. Others had been sold a lifetime membership and were demanding service. A few clients had never been matched at all. People were threatening to sue me. I had been able to sell easily for Soul Mates, but I had no confidence with Renaissance.

My husband gave up the church and came to work with me as matchmaker. Now he was dependent upon me. We spent countless hours talking, to dissatisfied clients to try to match them and comfort them.

I came to realize that something had happened to me which people fear the most. I had been conned.

Chapter 3   The Journey Upward

One night, after I bought Renaissance, I had a dream. I was on a stoneboat. A stoneboat is a flat surface, which is usually pulled by a horse. I was on the stoneboat moving upward. I went faster and faster, terrified out of my wits. I couldn't stop it or jump off, so I held on and kept moving. Finally I reached the top of the incline and the stoneboat stopped. There I could see a beautiful place where I had clear vision of the surroundings. I was at a ski lodge or such. I had a perfect view. Everything was clear and beautiful. This dream represented my life, which was a spiritual journey to a higher place.

Once the fear had gone, I was to reach a high place where I would have a calm, peaceful perspective. The dream frightened me, but it was a premonition of what my life would be like over the next few years.

Meanwhile, at the office, I was depressed, worried, and apprehensive. Very little money was coming in. Sandi had charged some clients a small monthly due to cover the costs of matching. These small cheques had helped me to pay some of the bills. I was not selling very much and the rent and other bills were piling up. My husband expected to be paid and of course had child support to pay.

I thought of my options. I needed a salary too and decided that since the business was my investment, I deserved to be paid. My husband had taken over, like he did in the church and was treating me like I was the secretary and he the proprietor. I decided to tell him to find a job elsewhere. With the rent due, I broke the news to him. He was angry and told me he had some place to go and he would talk to me later. I asked him to leave his key. I had fired him!

Then the truth hit me. I was left in my expensive office, many overheads to pay and a pile of rubble for clients. I did the only thing I could. I lay down on the floor and cried. St. Paul says that my power is made perfect in weakness. This must have been true for me because I stayed there for a while. Then I decided that I must go on. True, I had bought a lemon but I was not beat. I decided to try to turn it around. I got up and started to make a list of things I could do to improve my situation.

I decided to get rid of my two offices and talked to the property manager about a front office just for me. She had one and rented me a larger single office with white venetian blinds and a white desk. I had let go of having to pay my husband's salary and decided to cut down on some expensive advertising, which was not bringing me much business. My turning point must have worked because the phone started ringing with people wanting to know about the service and wanting to join.

My husband was looking through want ads when I got home and had gotten over his anger. The next day, he found a job in car leasing. I realized I had been enabling him to be helpless and dependent on me.

I took control of the business instead of letting it control me. It was always up and down but at least, I felt progress was being made.

Chapter 4   Twins

My favourite success story during my years at the agency was one of my earliest attempts at match making. This story blows apart any theories or beliefs that physical attractiveness, chemistry, chance, luck or numbers games have anything at all to do with finding a partner. The individual's beliefs, attitudes and approach are the deciding factors in getting what you want or so it would appear from my experience with Teddy and Terry, twin sisters, aged thirty-three.

Inseparable friends the two girls lived as roommates for twelve years without relationships, after leaving their parental home. Then for some unexplained reason they each decided it was time for marriage and a family. First Teddy joined the agency and about three months later then Terry, the week before I took it over. From my early experience with twin cousins and childhood friends, I knew that twins always wanted the same as each other. When Terry joined, her sister was already into a three-month relationship with an Indian doctor and wedding bells were being heard for the not too distant future.

Terry phoned us during our first week and said she had completed all her forms and was now ready to meet someone. "Why do I need an appointment?" she asked. "I know what I want." My husband, who was still working with me, explained that we had to meet her before we introduced her.

Reluctantly, she came in. A very average looking, slightly

overweight secretary, she seemed to have little going for her. Her appearance however, outweighed her personality. In a rude demanding tone she announced, "I want a doctor." As if that wasn't enough the doctor had to be young enough to put the kids through school before he died or retired. She also wanted a doctor who would be willing to leave his practice and travel or work in foreign countries for an extended period.

When asked what she had to give, she replied, "Well, I don't have AIDS." Terry was also clear that she was willing to play the role of doctor's wife and if he were from a foreign country she would cook whatever food he wanted or furnish the house in whatever fashion he chose. In other words, she was willing to do whatever it took to be a traditional wife to him.

When she left, we were bewildered. Ringing our hands, we thought, *Who does she think she is?* Imagine HER wanting a doctor! A week passed and there was no apparent solution to our dilemma. Then she called and asked, "Have you found him yet? Well I've decided not to be quite as fussy. I'll take anyone with a PH D."

It happened that in the files we found a young man with a PH D. Neil, a nuclear physicist of thirty-eight, visited the office on our invitation. Dressed in a plaid shirt, cords and runners he informed us he was a Nova Scotia farm boy. Spending most of his life at the books, he had achieved his doctorate in seven years, apparently quite a feat. Never having time for a relationship, he now found he was ready to marry.

When questioned about what he wanted he was not specific at all. She didn't need to be attractive or slim. Education was not important to him as long as she was intelligent. And yes he wanted a family and as for travelling to foreign countries, he did that with his present job. Feeling this to be too good to be true, I then asked the clincher "What about someone who is a bit on the aggressive side, someone who would perhaps take the lead?"

"Well sure, " he replied with a quiet smile. "I'm a bit the other way, so that would be great."

Not believing our luck, we made the introduction. We waited in suspense, wondering the outcome. After three months my curiosity got the best of me and I phoned him at work. Like all clients who were content, he was brief, anxious to end the conversation. I did understand him to say that everything was going well.

There was no further news until the following autumn, one year after the introduction. Then out of the blue, I received a phone call from Teddy, the other twin. She told me that Terry and Neil had been married that summer, had had a beautiful fairy tale wedding and were the proud owners of a new home. Everything had gone perfectly for Terry but Teddy's relationship with the Indian physician was on the rocks. She had called to see if I had anyone like Neil for her. I did! There was another young man named Humphery, whom I had kept on reserve for Terry should Neil not work out. Humphery was also a scientist, an introverted, sweet guy that none of the female clients liked because he was too quiet. He had received countless introductions but they had all rejected him on the grounds that he did not talk enough. It was like counselling one of them reported.

Teddy left her doctor on a Friday night, met Humphery the following Sunday and never looked back. They both called to put their files on hold during the month that followed. I remember saying to my husband, "Humphery doesn't know it yet, but he is getting married." The wedding occurred the following spring.

Humphery and Teddy stayed in touch. One day, they dropped by the office. They appeared so dedicated and devoted to each other, I just had to ask, "You went about this very logically, what about the emotional and physical side of the relationship?" They both smiled shyly and replied, "It's all there." I deduced that love is everywhere and when we find someone who is truly compatible, then love is there too. We don't have to fall in it.

Chapter 5   The Middle Years

As I look back in retrospect, Renaissance is nothing more that a blur, five years of being immersed in a struggle to survive, to prevent being swept under and to pay bills both personal and business expenses. As I said before it was also five years of forced personal growth and maturation.

From what I can remember, after a few months I settled into a routine at the office, at least as close as one could get to anything structured. It never ceased to be a roller coaster existence moving from one extreme to the other: slow to busy, optimism to hopelessness, satisfying to frustrating and back again.

I virtually did everything. My job consisted of advertising and marketing, promoting, selling, counselling, interviewing, match making, paying bills and answering phones. Most of the telephone calls were people wanting information about the service. I regretted having to do this, but I found I had to constantly exaggerate the number of clients I had. I never volunteered the number and tried to evade the question if it came up, but I realized I would never sell a membership if I told the truth about actual number of active clients I had. I discovered that while I exaggerated by a few hundred, other agencies were exaggerating by thousands. After a while I developed a script, which I became very comfortable with but which was not memorized. I would try to get them to commit to an appointment. If I didn't succeed, I would try to get their address and I would mail them a brochure. If I could get them to give me their phone number, then I would add their names to a list of leads, which I would call them again and follow up. The lead list proved to be a valuable sales tool.

Once I got them into the office, I then would try to soft sell them, mainly on my knowledge, my integrity, my honesty, my warmth, and me. I came to realize that this was what my agency had that others did not-me. I would ask them to be realistic about their chances without at the same time scare them away. I did scare some away. I would later find out that some of them went right out and joined another agency, where they were not informed of the reality of their chances. What usually happened was that they would meet with failure at the other agency and eventually return to me. This could take six months, one year or maybe even three years but in time most of them returned. I learned that as time went on I stopped beating myself up for losing a sale.

If I were, successful in signing up a client, they would pay, sign a contract and go home with the forms to fill out on themselves and their preferences. They would then return with the completed forms and I would have a second interview with them and possibly show them some potential files. The ultimate choice was theirs and I would record people whom they refused and who refused them. I also recorded all matches made and all successful ones, which I considered to be three months or more together.

When I wasn't selling or interviewing, I would use my time to match people, starting with a list of men and a list of women who needed a match. Then I would go through their respective files until I found something that looked like reasonable compatibility. Then I would start phoning, talking to answering machines and being called back. Some of them would come in to look at profiles and photos while others trusted my judgement completely. As I got them matched, I would cross them off the list, but sometimes I would be up against brick walls as they refused people or met someone in the interim or disappeared on me. There were some who were difficult and would remain on the match list for weeks at a time. When I found myself really stuck, I contacted other agencies and we would do some cross agency matching. However, most of these matches didn't work out as matches from other agencies irritated some clients. I also tried giving away free memberships to age groups, which were scarce, such as older men. I found too that matches to those who had not paid a fee had made no personal commitment, rarely worked out.

Also in my spare time, I would follow up leads, calling people back who phoned for information. Some were people who had been in for an interview but had not joined. Some were people who had been to my information night. Many calls were unsuccessful at the time but many would remember my call and phone in weeks, months or even years later ready to join.

Some days were busy - others were quiet. Some months I almost starved and others were plentiful. There were few predictable trends. Generally speaking, it was quiet just before and just after statutory holidays. December, January and June were usually busy. February, May and November were generally slow. Summer proved to be busy when one could expect people to be on holidays. There was nothing I could count on.

I came to let go of any expectations. Some days heavily booked would result in cancellations, no shows and bomb outs. Other days when nothing was scheduled would turn out to be productive and profitable.

I came to realize how helpless I was in the business. It seemed to have nothing to do with the amount of advertising I did, the number of leads I called, how much I prayed and asked others to pray for me or the number of positive affirmations I made or goals I had written. All seemed futile. If business was down, it was down. At times with bills piling up, the rent due and no appointments booked, I would be ready to pack it in. When in a depressed hopeless state it would suddenly shift. I would then get caught up and a little ahead and hope would be restored. I would just begin to think I had discovered the secret to success, when it would go into another slump. At times, I was seriously disillusioned and other times I was confident, elated and living in faith. I came to accept the unpredictability of this business.

In spite of my hopes that I could build it up and sell it, it remained much the same over the five years that I had it. A shift did occur, however, but that shift was in me. In those first few months, I remembered being terrified when there was a complaint. I was frequently called a crook, threatened being reported to the Better Business Bureau, or worse yet, legal action. People, whose contracts were very old and had paid the previous owners, were demanding refunds. I took it all as a personal attack, feeling guilty, ashamed and tainted.

As time progressed, I came to realize that these angry people had always been angry. They had always found someone to blame for their unhappiness that I just happened to be their target at that particular time. I learned that many of my clients were actually dysfunctional people, co-dependents who were incapable of having a normal, healthy relationship. As these realizations were slowly assimilated into my mind and emotions, I began to handle these calls in a different way. I told them I was sorry they felt that way. I stopped feeling like I had done something disgusting by introducing them to someone they didn't like. I realized some of them didn't like anyone particularly themselves.

One way to eliminate old clients from years before from coming back and demanding service or a refund, was to weed the files. We kept files for everyone who had joined within the past two years and the older files were put into green garbage bags and ritualistically thrown into the trash. I remember feeling a few pangs of guilt when this was done but it was short lived. After that, if old clients called, they were told that there was no file on them, but they were most welcome to join if they wished. In order to receive service, they had to produce a current contract, complete all the new forms and attend a seminar for new members. Only one person complied with these conditions.

I got so I was no longer willing to take a lot of verbal abuse from people on the telephone. If they did not speak to me civilly, I would refuse to talk to them and often hung up on them. Many would call back and apologize for their behavior the next day. They found out that the first thing they had to do if they wanted service was to be nice to me.

In the beginning, most of the complaints were about the previous owner. Countless people felt like I did, that they had been ripped off. Eventually this attitude of contempt was replaced by something else. As old clients became less vocal and my own clients became more prevalent, the contempt mellowed out. In less than two years I can only describe what clients felt for me was respect and awe. Highly educated and professional people came to treat me as their equal. I came to be seen as a professional.

My confidence came as a process. With the help of my husband, despite his faults, we drew up new forms, revising and improving them as we went along. We wrote up a new contract, which spelled everything in black and white, so that no one could claim they were deceived. In this contract they agreed to be reasonable and realistic. They agreed that there were no refunds and that they could be suspended for unethical behaviour. We developed our own seminar for new members attempting to enlighten them on the realistic truths about relationships and asking them to let go of unrealistic expectations. My growth in the business was a gradual evolution.

For the first year, I entered the office in a great deal of fear, wondering what sort of peril would await me there. I dreaded receiving messages and mail for fear they might be abusive. In the five years I had the business, I never quite got over that fear. This fear was fed when one of the previous owner's clients sued me and won. I will deal with that later.

Not all my days were filled with disaster. Over the five yeas, I was able to make some very successful matches. Some of them married and some did not. Some broke up again. Many of the happy people disappeared into oblivion. Three couples invited me to their weddings. Many others sent me cards, photos, wedding announcements and thank yous. I was invited to dinner at some of their homes and others became permanent friends. I began a scrapbook of successes, which I used as a sales tool, and a very effective one at that.

An event occurred after my first year and a half, which was to be the ultimate test of my tenacity and strength. In May of 1991, I left my husband. The breakup had nothing to do with the business but was the result of his continued abuse toward me. The split left me devastated, grief stricken and alone at a time when the business was in a slump. Feeling financially insecure, heartbroken and betrayed, I found an apartment and went through the hassle of moving. My feelings also included abandonment, being unsupported and vulnerable. Feeling as though there was nothing else in my life, I threw myself into my work. My fears were unwarranted as I found immediately when I claimed back my power, the business picked up.

One change I was to implement was the seminar for new members into an information night for potential clients. Instead of trying to change members, I decided to focus my attention on recruiting new clients. This proved to be a valuable sales technique. I presented the seminar by myself, and gained further confidence as I always had my husband to depend on in the past. I had the brochure redone to eliminate my husband from the advertising.

Chapter 6   The Kidney Transplant People

An unusual match was made with a couple who were matched not on the basis of their hearts but instead their kidneys.

Karen came to me first. She was a young teacher who was on disability leave because she was waiting for a kidney donor. She was very relaxed about it and not worried at all. I told her she was in a difficult situation because many men would not want to meet someone with an illness. She was willing to take her chances.

Jim joined shortly after. He was also at a disadvantage for many reasons: he was from out of town, he was short, had children from a previous marriage and he was a recovering alcoholic. However, he was willing to meet Karen, in spite of her situation. He told me had a sister who was waiting for a kidney and that he was a potential donor. He was actually enthused about meeting Karen in spite of her illness. Karen agreed to meet him and he left with the names of three women who had said yes to meeting him. I wished him well.

A few weeks later, Jim and Karen came into the office to let me know what had happened. They had met and hit it off right away and had plans to marry. He had met Karen first and had not called the other two women, whose numbers I had given him. Jim had donated a kidney to his sister, but Karen's surgery had not happened yet. Her brother had agreed to donate a kidney to her. What an unusual twist to the story!

A few months later I received a telephone message stating that Jim and Karen had been married and that she was in the hospital for transplant surgery. Later I heard from her friend that the transplant had not gone well but I lost touch with Karen and Jim and didn't find out the results.

Chapter 7   Decisions, Decisions

This chapter, I have devoted to outlining the content of my Information Night, which I perfected as a promotional tool for recruiting new clients. It was given from the heart with the intention of giving potential clients some insight into relationships. Because it was seminar material it is written in the present tense. It went something like this.

I have seen a great many clients since I have been in this business. In spite of the difficulty of keeping in touch with happy people, I have been able to work out some statistics on my success rate. It seems that once people are in a good relationship, I am the last person they want to hear from. To the best of my knowledge, these are the figures. First let me define what I mean by a relationship. I have come to consider a relationship something that has lasted for a three-month period. That allows for issues to come up that need to be confronted. Anything less than three months is casual dating. After three months, the relationship stands a chance of surviving, but of course may still break up after the three-month period. Back to the statistics, after three months at the agency, 35% of clients find themselves in a relationship. After one year, an additional 30% will find themselves in a relationship. At that time, there are still another 35% who are not in a relationship after countless introductions. Why is this happening and how can it change so that a larger number of clients can meet with success during our one-year membership?

Over the years at the agency, I have spoken to a lot of single people both as clients and people who telephone me for information. These people all have one thing in common. They are not in a relationship and would like to be. From my observations of them, they seem to fall into three categories. The first group are those who tell me that they never meet anyone. The second group are those who meet lots of people date a lot but nothing long term ever develops for them. The third category includes those who meet people, get into relationships easily but their relationships are full of pain and suffering. In other words, they are unable to have a healthy relationship. There seems to be a two-fold nature to this prevalent problem. There is difficulty getting into a relationship and an equal amount of difficulty maintaining it once one has begun.

Another characteristic which these three groups share is the fact that they are all making some type of excuse for why they are not successful in finding what they want. The first group will say that there are just no men or women out there, that is the reason for their singleness. The category, which can't find a relationship that, lasts more than a couple of weeks say they haven't met the right person yet. The third group will tell you the world is so full of losers that is all they meet. The world or something outside of themselves is the cause of their singleness. As long as it is the world's fault, we are powerless to change it.

It is my belief, that it is not the world's fault but the fault of the individual. This may be difficult to accept. The good news about this theory is if that we are each responsible for what we are getting, then we have the power to change it. It is also my belief that the end result of what we get in life is the sum total of our beliefs, attitudes and past conditioning. Let us assume that I am right. We can examine the three types of singles under this new assumption.

To return to category one, those who never meet anyone, let us examine another possible reason for their situation. If they are themselves responsible for this happening, then perhaps the real reason they are not meeting anyone is maybe deep down they don't really want to. On the surface, they consciously say they want a relationship, but underneath there may be FEAR. These people may have been seriously hurt at one time or they have never recovered the loss of a past relationship or they simply may not be ready. I also come across clients who were too busy to meet anyone. There was simply no room in their lives for anyone. So of course, they would not meet anyone.

Because they are not ready, they are not sending out any vibes that they are receptive and may be saying nonverbally "stay away." One client told me that she only met men when she was on vacation. It was then that she was probably open. Anyone who wants a relationship must be ready or no attempts will work. If you aren't meeting anyone then you are most likely not ready. You must make a conscious choice to have a relationship. With forty-two per cent of Vancouver's population being single and of this group fifty percent being male and the other fifty percent being female, it seems impossible that there is just no one out there to meet.

To return to the second group, those who date large numbers but each relationship lasts only for a short time. What is the real reason for not meeting anyone? How many do they need to meet? I recently watched a television program where a counsellor was answering questions about men who won't commit to a relationship. She told of a bachelor who was a compulsive dater and over a period of time had dated about two thousand women. She said that being unable to commit in a relationship is a way of life. When asked how do you get such a man to commit she said you couldn't. You are wasting your time trying.

Getting back to category two, how many people do you have to meet before you find the right one? How many years will it take? I will put forth a more realistic reason why category two is meeting with failure. They are doing so because they don't know what the right person for them is. They haven't defined what they really want so of course they won't recognize it if it dropped in their laps. They hold a fantasy of a perfect partner. Such a person doesn't exist. I know a client is fantasizing when I get a request from a woman who wants a rich man who is willing to spend a lot of time with her or a man who wants a woman who is erotic and sensuous and at the same time a virgin.

These are unlikely combinations. A fantasy may be standing in your way of a relationship. The belief that it is a numbers game is proven incorrect at Renaissance. From my experience with clients is that the successful ones, actually met very few people. I have a number of clients who married the first person they met. So you see it really has little to do with numbers.

Now for category three: those who always have bad relationships. Perhaps the real reason may be they are attracting partners based on some early conditioning during their childhood, A woman who always attracts alcoholics may be subconsciously looking for "Dad" who was alcoholic or had some other addiction. This category of people may have more difficulty overcoming their problem than the other two groups but it is not impossible. Some therapy, a twelve step program or some workshops may be necessary before this person becomes more aware of his or her mistakes in making choices,

Let us assume that my reasoning is correct, as to why people are not successful. I will devote my next chapter to what can be done to change it.

Chapter 8 Decisions Part II

What can we change about ourselves in order to change our lives? I believe it is a matter of making certain decisions about our lives. It is about taking control. In Raymond Charles Barker's book, *The Power of Decision*, he tells us that no decision is a decision to fail. He also tells us that those people who have no goals in life end up helping others to achieve their goals.

I would like to interject with an example from my own life. My Siamese cat had been killed. I felt terrible but decided I would wait a year before I chose to get another cat. After all there are advantages to being pet less. However after about four months, I realized that I really did want another cat, that I didn't need a year to know that. I didn't however decide when I wanted it. Would you believe that I had a cat the next day? My husband, who had not known of my decision, decided I needed a cat and got me one at the SPCA.

At this point in the seminar, I would tell the story of the twins as told in a previous chapter. The story of the twins demonstrates the power of decision and disproves any beliefs that success in finding a relationship has anything to do with luck, chance, physical attractiveness or numbers games. Based on this story, I have come up with four basic decisions that one must make in order to be successful.

The first decision is simply making a decision to have a relationship. The twins had each decided that she wanted to get married. Then each had gone out and joined the agency in order to make it happen for her. Before anyone can make that decision, they must be ready. I can tell if they are not ready, if they take months to fill out their forms or if they reject every introduction on the basis of some petty detail, such as he's too tall or too short, too something. The ready people are anxious to join, to put their money on my desk, to sign a contract and to complete the forms. They are excited to get on with the process. The interesting thing is that because they have made a commitment, they start meeting people all over the place.

Decision two is about what one wants. The twins knew exactly what they wanted. They were both perfectly clear that they wanted to be traditional wives, so therefore they required certain qualities on the part of the men in order to have that lifestyle. In order to know what one wants, we need to know a lot about ourselves, the lifestyle we want, what our long-term goals are and also what our standards and boundaries are. If having a family is a goal, as it was with the twins, then we must have a partner who has that goal as well. The counsellor I mentioned earlier, said you can't change a noncommittal man. You must look for someone who wants what you do.

Knowing and being able to define your standards is essential in finding the right partner. There are standards for everything else in life, for driving an automobile, for university entrance, building, safety and health standards, but we somehow feel we don't have the right to standards in relationships. Standards and boundaries mean being aware of what types of behaviour we are willing or not willing to tolerate from our partner. This includes such issues as money standards, morality, sexuality, cleanliness, honesty and habits such as smoking or alcohol use. If we are not aware and have not defined our own standards, we cannot expect the other person to know what they are. What often happens is we meet someone and get into a relationship and then discover they do something we don't like. Then we mistakenly think we can change him or her.

To summarize decision two, you must know what it is you want. We make decisions about everything else, what clothes to buy, what career we want, where we want to live. Why do we feel we haven't the right to choose what type of relationship we want?

At the agency, we get you to define as specifically as possible what you want in terms of qualities and standards. Would you phone Sears and tell them to send you something nice? No! You would describe exactly what you wanted or risk getting something you don't want or even like. When defining what it is you want it is important to consider your lifestyle and your own values. Adhere strictly to the items that are really important to you and forget the trivial items that are not going to make a difference to your life. When you know what you want, you will recognize it when you see it. If you want a red Toyota car, then you will not waste a lot of energy and time, test-driving green Chevys. When you know what sort of person you want, you don't need to date two thousand people in order to find that person.

I always give the example of myself, when I was looking for roommates for my condo. I would take anyone who applied, not provide any house rules and get very angry when they didn't do everything the way I did. Then I would end up kicking them out. This happened several times until I realized I was doing everything backwards. I should have started with a list of standards and presented them to the potential renters. If anyone objected, then I would know they were the wrong person. That way I would have only taken suitable tenants who knew where they stood with me. You see, people respect you for your standards and by having standards you save yourself a lot of grief, time and effort.

Decision three is the decision to be willing to do whatever it takes to have your relationship. This may mean you have to give up something, to change something in your life. It means also being aware of what you are and are not willing to give up. And it means, knowing what it is you have to give in a relationship. There is no receiving without giving. What does all this mean? The twins knew what they had to give. Each one was willing to be a traditional wife and to do whatever it took to be just that. Knowing what we are willing and able to give up means that we must be willing to give up some of our activities in order to make time for the other person. I have many clients who are so busy they could not possibly fit another person into their schedule. These clients are often women. One woman in particular was a bank executive. The man she met was very interested in her, but she was always too busy to see him, so eventually he gave up. You must be willing to perhaps work less, see your children less, see your mother less or ski less. The third decision means making the relationship a priority.

Let me caution you about this decision. There is a fine line between giving up something to make room for a relationship and giving up too much. If it means giving up who and what you are, then you are probably giving up too much. Women are often guilty of this too. One woman wanted her relationship to work so badly that she gave up all her activities, her friends, and started spending all of her time hiking, because that is what her partner did. She ended up selling out to the man. My second husband hated cats and when we were married, I had a cat. He agreed to accept the cat because he wanted me but he resented every moment that cat was in the house and he never let me forget it for a minute. He had given too much. If you have to give up too much of who you are in a relationship, then it is probably wrong for you. In a right relationship, it must be easy to give up something. In fact it should not feel like a sacrifice at all.

I mentioned before that everyone has something to give. In a healthy relationship, there is giving and receiving. One client I inherited from another agency came to my office to visit me one day. When asked what he wanted, he stated his wants in not uncertain terms. She had to be amorous. Amorous! He kept reiterating that word. I assumed he meant willing to have sex at the drop of a hat. She had to be beautiful, tall, long blond hair, slim, a model's body. She also needed to be earning $60,000 per year and not be interested in marriage or children.

I said, "A woman like that is very special. What do you have to give?"

He replied, "I gave in my last relationship."

I mentioned this in one of my seminars. I asked the group. "Who do you think would fit his description? I can't think of anyone."

One quiet lady in the audience, replied, "Maybe a hooker." It appeared he had come to the wrong agency. To return to giving, what you gave in your last relationship doesn't count!

We all have something special to give. It can be love, support, caring, sharing, nurturing, empowerment. You need to take stock of what your gift is. Make sure it is something you are willing and able to give.

The first three decisions are about finding the right relationship. Decision four is about keeping that relationship once you are in it. We, at the agency will provide help and support if you run into difficulty. We recognize that no relationship is without conflict. In a healthy relationship, issues can be confronted, solutions and compromised reached. If you are in category three, and you always seem to have tumultuous relationships, you may need some help. You may need to do some extra personal growth work on yourself to heal old self-defeating patterns.

You may come to a place in your relationship where you are not sure is it is right for you. I do not give advice but I may ask you to get in touch with what is right for you. I will ask you to look at what it is that is troubling you. Sometimes we have unrealistic expectations of the other person or of the relationship itself. Let us back up a few steps. What is the difference between an expectation and a standard? A standard is a clearly defined law about what is acceptable and what is not. An expectation is a wish usually unexpressed about some change we think our partner should make.

The twins had standards. They knew they wanted educated men with the stability and traditional values which those qualities would bring them. They had no expectations about changing their man after they were married. They did not plan to change his looks, dress or personality. The twins were totally willing to accept their man the way he was. You see, many of us go for stability and then choose someone who cannot give us that. Neither did the twins have any ideas about changing themselves in order to get what they wanted. They had no thoughts that if they lost twenty pounds and bleached their hair, then maybe they could have a doctor.

Getting back to how I can help you if things aren't going the way you want them to. I may ask you if you have unrealistic expectations of your partner. If so, can you let go of your expectations? If you cannot and your partner cannot change, then get out. It's that simple.

I will give you an example of an unrealistic expectation. One client said she always expected flowers on the second date. If she didn't get them, then that was the end of the relationship. That was her standard, but because the men knew nothing about it, it was an expectation. Your partner cannot read your mind!

One young lady, who was in a six-month relationship, called one day and wanted to see me. After talking with her, I discovered she was feeling uncomfortable with her partner's inability to commit. When she asked him what he wanted he would say, "I want you." She clearly wanted marriage and a family, but was feeling she didn't have the right to ask what his intentions were. She thought perhaps six months was too soon. She kept blaming herself for what she considered discomfort with his constant reference to his previous relationship. I told her that of course she had a right to know what he wanted. If his intentions were not the same as hers, then she needed to know before she had invested any more time, energy and emotion in the relationship. I also told her to tell him about her discomfort with his habit of talking about his past. I told her to let him know it bothered her and ask him if cares about her not to do it. I told her also that she needed to take a risk. It may mean the end of the relationship but it would be better that spending another six months wondering and then breaking up. She left my office confident in confronting him. A couple of weeks later I called to see how things were and she assured me everything was fine this time.

Another young man phoned me after a yearlong relationship with a woman. They were spiritual people and he especially followed a group called Si Baba and had travelled to India. He sought a relationship with a spiritual woman who was willing to have a family. The lady in question was not that interested in having a family. She had been spending more and more time studying to be a pharmacist through night school. Each time they planned an activity, she took her books along to study. Growing tired of this scenario, he would request that she make some time for the two of them. She would agree and then without his knowledge, sign up for another semester. As they approached forty, he believed there would never be an appropriate time

I gave him the same advice that was offered to me during a crucial time in my life. I told him that first he had to tell her what he wanted. If she couldn't give him that then he needed to make two lists. The first list would include the advantages to staying in the relationship. The second list would include the advantages of leaving. If the first list exceeded the second, then he must forgive. If the second list was greater then the next step was divorce with joy. He thanked me kindly and said he would do just that. One week later he called for another introduction. This time I had a young woman who was also involved in eastern religions and had been a nun in an eastern tradition. They were married in an eastern tradition. One day I met them in a supermarket and they introduced me to their two month old son, Rama, who I am sure is destined to be a guru.

Not all relationships are right. Some of them can be worked out. Others need to be dispensed with and we need to start over again. I will hopefully help you to get touch with what is right for you.

What does all this mean? It means to ask yourself the four questions mentioned above briefly, they are:

1. Do you want a relationship?
2. If so what do you want? What kind of person do you want? What are your standards?
3. What do you have to give in a relationship?
4. Are you willing to have a healthy relationship?

If you can answer yes to these questions, then please make an appointment with me. One final comment: You are probably wondering about love. Where does it fit in? You can make a conscious choice about your relationship and still have love. The twins did.

You see, falling in love is one of life's great illusions! M. Scott Peck in his book The Road Less Travelled 2 tells us that falling in love is nature's way of tricking us into having children so that the human race goes on. Falling in love is always followed by falling out of love. Have you ever heard of anyone staying in that initial, beautiful, starry-eyed state forever? Have you? I doubt if anyone ever has because falling in love always brings us the opposite, which is pain. The best we can hope for is that it will mellow out into a mutual respect and mutually beneficial support system. If we merely rely on falling in love to find a partner, we risk getting someone who doesn't meet our standards and with whom we can't live. My clients talk a lot about chemistry. Chemistry is important but we cannot base our choice of mate on that alone. Do you know the real definition of passion? It means suffering. Do you want suffering in your relationship or do you want joy? A beautiful face, body or great sex is not going to add a thing to a time of crisis and tragedy in you life, but a loving giving partner can help you through it.

When choosing your mate, make sure it is a conscious

choice to love for better or for worse. If it turns out to be worse then you will have all the love and support that it takes to face the problem.

1. Barker, Raymond Charles, The Power of Decision, Dodd Mead & Company,
1968
2. M. Scott Peck, The Road Less Travelled, Simon and Schuster, New York 1978, pages 84-90

Chapter 9　The Yellow Ribbon

In her hair, she wears a yellow ribbon.
She wears it in the springtime
And in the month of May.
　And if you ask her why the heck she wears it.
She wears it for her lover,
　Who is far, far away.

Among some clients transferring from another agency was an educated professional woman of about fifty years. I perused her file, which arrived by mail, finding it filled with "has been" photos of herself as a young woman. Plainly she had been a beauty, a slim brunet with deep sensitive eyes and a sweet smile. Strategically hidden among these photos, there was one shot of an older Slavic featured woman with brassy colored hair. Clearly, this was a recent photo so placed on the page that the viewer would not notice the difference time had made.

In the section of the form, where she had defined her wants, well perfection was perhaps a modest description. She had rejected a number of men and thus far had met no one at the other agency. Mentally, I slotted her as one of the "picky."

On the telephone, in a European accented voice, she asked to come in and look at any prospects I might have. When she came in, she provided me with a cut out from a magazine, an advertisement for Calvin Klein. It depicted a couple dressed in swimming attire, reclining on a beach, clutched in a sensuous embrace. The man in the advertisement, an obvious gorgeous hunk, had been her previous mate and that is what she again sought. From her handbag, she took another snapshot of the same man. When I asked her to put into words what it was she wanted, she could only verbalize a physical description. "Tall, fit, handsome, a tennis player's body, youthful, well dressed, a full head of hair," were the words she used. When I questioned her about the qualities of the soul, she looked at me with those doe like eyes, as if I had three heads.

She kept returning to the photo in her purse. When I asked her about the man in the photo, she told me she had tolerated seven years of abuse, unfaithfulness and alcoholism from this man, whom she had financially supported. When I told her to throw out the photo, that holding on to it was keeping her from having a relationship; she looked at me again with those sensitive eyes and quickly dropped the treasured item back into her purse.

In my attempts to match her, I never found anyone who met her standards and none of my desirable male clients were interested in meeting her. Here was a lost soul, searching and longing for the gigolo who abused her and at the same time rejecting any semblance of a healthy relationship. As she left my office, that day I am sure I caught a glimpse of something yellow in that brassy hair!

Chapter 10   The Gender Gap: How To Bring Us Closer

This chapter is an article which I wrote for a single's magazine and which was published in an edited form. This is the unabridged edition.

The battle of the sexes goes on! Both men and women are voicing their concerns, each accusing the other of being immature, egotistical or manipulative. The truth is the two sexes are both seeking the same end - love, intimacy and companionship. Why can't the differences be put aside and the end result be reached? Well, that can happen, but it involves trying to understand where it is coming from.

There are basic differences in the sexes, some are biological and others are socially and cultural based. In the beginning, the goal of male and female interaction was procreation and its purpose was survival. The objective of the male was to impregnate the female, while the female gave birth and cared for her young. Both the female and the young required food, shelter and protection provided by the male. The prerequisites for the female was that she be attractive enough to allow him to have an erection and an orgasm and that she be of child-bearing age. The male had to be physically strong and aggressive to eliminate other males and to hunt for food and to provide protection from predators.

Today, relationships are no longer contingent upon procreation or for that matter, procreation upon relationships. Men and women's roles are overlapping and interchanging. One of the problems is that our basic criteria for selecting a mate is still the same as primitive mans rather than based upon present reality. Dr. Warren Farrel in his book, *Why Men are the Way They Are* 3, claims that man's primary motivation in seeking a relationship is sex, while a woman's is commitment. Men are still seeking young beautiful bodies and women a strong powerful provider. This claim is supported by my observations at the agency. Young beautiful women and high achieving, tall men are in demand. This means there are many older, less attractive women and younger, less established men in non-prestigious jobs, experiencing difficulty in finding partners. Why have our methods of choosing partners not kept up with the times?

In Ken Keyes's book, *How To Enjoy Life In Spite Of It All* 4, he claims that all human suffering comes from three basic addictions: POWER, SENSATION AND SECURITY! Addictions are always based on a feeling of emptiness from within. Therefore, regardless of how much of the three we get, it is never enough. We continue to feel empty.

In the light of Keyes's assumption, let us look at how these addictions affect our choice of partners. Let us suppose a woman is seeking emotional and financial support from a relationship with a man. She may also receive a sensation or a feeling of power through being connected with a powerful man. Because of the time involved in being successful and the stresses inherent with job performance, she rarely sees her man and when she does, they do not communicate. She discovers that she has sacrificed intimacy for security and is consequently lonely and unhappy. She may look elsewhere for the sensations that eliminate the emptiness, such as alcohol, drugs or extra-marital affairs. She discovers that a man's performance as a provider has little to do with his ability to communicate and to give her the sensations she wants.

Similarly, a man seeking the sensation of having a young and beautiful woman at his disposal, may also receive a sense of power and security in possessing her. The pressure on him to perform better is soon felt as he strives to please her, keep her attention and support the family they have created in the style he promised This requires more time at work and less chance to receive the affection and sex he sought in the beginning. As we well know young beautiful women eventually become older, less beautiful and sometimes more demanding. As he is distanced from his original goal he is likely to seek the sensations and power that he needs elsewhere, alcohol, compulsive spending, gambling or other more beautiful women.

Returning to Keyes, he claims seeking any of the three addictions always bring us pain. We can see how men and women sabotage the very thing they seek. As a result, no one's needs are being met.

Often I find in my service that many people are seeking in another person what they themselves feel they are lacking. Those who are overweight are looking for someone who is slim. Those who feel old and ugly are looking for youth and beauty. The weak seek strength. The poor are after financial security. Ultimately the insecure person with low self-esteem finds another like himself. In other words, men and women alike are motivated out of their sense of incompleteness and end up with more of the same. The answer lies in self-acceptance looking within oneself rather than to others for fulfillment.

Let us have another look at primitive man and woman. He was aggressive, strong, powerful and fearless. She was passive, gentle and vulnerable. The truth is we all are created whole, each possessing a feminine and masculine side. Society has discouraged men from expressing their feelings or being soft and gentle. Women are discouraged from being aggressive. By realizing our own androgyny, we can become more balanced emotionally, physically and mentally thereby increasing our chances of attracting a likewise balanced mate.

Another way to realize our wholeness is by surrendering our addiction to sensation. Like overcoming any addiction this can be difficult. Let me explain. Many of my clients have as their goal, a sensation known as chemistry, passion or falling in love. Not to undermine the need for physical attraction, I again refer to M. Scott Peck's work, which I have referred to earlier in this book. He states that falling in love is one of life's many little tricks to get us to propagate the race. It doesn't last! It isn't meant to. There must be something deeper to sustain a relationship through time and crises.

Confirming Peck's claim, I have some clients who seek excitement and end up in a failed relationship. These people are often attractive and successful in other areas of their lives. The happy clients, who meet with a successful match, are usually looking for a real person not a sensational one.

In conclusion, in order to come together successfully in a relationship, men and women must give up searching for their completeness in others. What someone can do for us is the wrong reason for choosing a partner?

What can you do to find wholeness? First examine your own behaviour and activities and evaluate. How much if your behaviour is motivated by power, sensation or security? Know this truth. We have within us the power to create a life for ourselves, with all the security we need. There are no sensations that equal the joy of self-acceptance, unconditional love and faith in oneself.

Next practice at becoming balanced within yourself, recognizing both your masculine and feminine qualities, integrating and assimilating these two powerful sides of yourself into wholeness. I often visualize my masculine and feminine loving, nurturing and supporting each other.

Lastly, stop looking for sensations like falling in love. It's a lot like giving up the belief in Santa Claus. It hurts a little at first and then you start believing in yourself. I believe that when you love yourself, others will love you too. You see it is a choice not an accident. Finally, I ask you to give up your search for perfections in others but instead to look inside yourself for that wonderful unique person that you are. Only then will you attract some one who is whole also. By working towards this end, men and women can hopefully achieve harmony with each other.

3. Farrel, Dr. Warren, "Why Men Are The Way They Are."
4. Keyes, Ken Jr. "How To Enjoy Your Life In Spite Of It All" Love Line Books, Oregon. 1980,

Chapter 11   Dreamers Versus Seekers

From my experience at the agency, I came to know and understand the differences between people who were fantasizing or day dreaming about the perfect partner and those who were creatively visualizing what they wanted. There were basic differences in the process and very different results. I will attempt to describe the characteristics of each and then to give examples of real people who fit into both.

Dreaming probably started when the person was very young. Many families are not very happy: children are not always loved the way they would like to be. The child fantasizes about having a wonderful family or person who would love him the way they long to be loved. Everything is perfect in this daydream. It may be the only source of pleasure the unfortunate child may have. Dreams like this continue into late childhood, adolescence and adulthood, only now it is a fantasy about a perfect love, who is always beautiful, loving, gentle, loyal compliant and kind. Pleasure and comfort come from this dream. The dreamer is searching continually for this perfect person. At times the dreamer seems to find the dream, but upon discovering some human flaw in the real person, they then reject the person, knowing their dream person would never be so tainted. Dreamers will eventually find that no one lives up to the dream. No one ever can since that is all it is – a dream. Life becomes an endless search for this person. One disappointment follows another. The dream person who is found may reject the dreamer who can then continue to long for the one who got away. Unrequited love is the plight of the dreamer, who may never recover from the loss. Because he holds on to his dream of perfection, no one will ever measure up to it.

How is having a fantasy different from knowing what we want? The person who knows what he wants, I shall call for lack of a better word, a seeker. This person is aware of what human qualities he would like to have in his partner and has assimilated them into his reality. The dreamer, on the hand is acting outside of reality and has created a super human being as his goal.

Female dreamers usually fantasize about rich powerful men who are dashing, handsome, beguiling, fascinating, totally devoted, exciting and honest. Real human traits, which a rich powerful man may possess, such as workaholism, ruthlessness, miserliness are not included in the fantasy. If men are exciting with one woman, they may be to all women. The female dreamer will be attracted to such men, but when she discovers that her man also possesses the less desirable qualities, she will reject her man. He doesn't match her dream. The woman ends up hurt, disappointed and longing for her real partner again. As long as she clings to her dream, she keeps having the same experience.

Male fantasizers are searching endlessly for a face - a young beautiful face and a slim willowy perfectly formed body. One dreamer even brought me a picture of a woman's face cut from a magazine. As well as being beautiful, the dream woman must be sweet, kind, passive, nurturing, loyal and admiring of him. Male dreamers are looking for a doll combining virginity and eroticism at the same time, something like a show pony, an angel, a mermaid, a whore, a baby and a mother all in one. If the dreamer meets such a woman, she is often not interested in him and like his female counterpart, the male dreamer ends up hurt and longing again for the dream.

While the goal of a seeker is a life style the goal of a dreamer is an emotional high, a sensation. The reasons for rejecting someone are no chemistry, not being physically attractive enough, too fat, eyes too small or bad bite. They rarely cite such reasons, as the person is not stable enough or too phoney. Dreamers are usually attracted to shallow people because they are looking for a superficial exterior and have not looked beneath the outer layer.

The problem is that most dreamers are not aware they are

dreaming. Their dreams may appear to them to be creative visualization. How can one identify a fantasy? I have tried to define the difference as follows. A fantasy moves acts and speaks in a way that is prescribed by the dreamer. He controls the fantasy. It does what he wants. A seeker gives no face or personality to the visualization. It is a clear idea of what he wants- faceless, voiceless, frozen, unmoving. The seeker then allows his vision to take whatever form it will a long as it represents those human qualities he has envisioned.

The dreamer constantly retreats into a motion picture account of numerous events of a fairy tale nature, which include such emotions as excitement, ecstasy, pleasure, comfort and anticipation. The seeker on the other hand visualized his mate and releases the whole idea, knowing it will take form as he had defined it. There is no emotion and no script.

I came to recognize the differences in clients after they had met with introductions, which were unsuccessful. The dreamer compares everyone with his fantasy. Most everyone falls short. Dreamers are critical and angry each time they meet with a disappointment. A seeker seems to evaluate each person, looking for the qualities he seeks. He realizes everyone is human and he finds each one unique and interesting even if they are not the right one. When he finds someone who meets his requirements, he recognizes this person as being a potential mate.

John was a dreamer. He had everything going for him, looks, height (six, four) success, brains and money. Everything was wonderful in his life from his BMW to his townhouse in False Creek-everything except a relationship. John was an unhappy man.

From a deep sensitive emotional temperament, he masked his feelings in a harsh analysis of life in general. He came to the agency requesting a tall, extremely attractive, slim gorgeously sexy woman. Attractive was not enough. She had to be out of this world. The interesting thing was that he had never had a relationship with a woman like that. All of previous relationships were with very ordinary women who had ultimately become friends with John. His one meaningful relationship was a brief encounter with a critical woman who had abused his sensitive nature and had eventually married someone else.

Only one woman at the agency was to meet his standards. John courted Sue for about six weeds before she broke up with him. John was inadvertently looking for shallowness in a woman and that is what he found. Sue's reasons for breaking up with him included his not being physically attractive enough, his moustache, hair, his car, and his intensity. John ended up being judged by his own standards.

John was a classic example of a dreamer. His fantasy of the perfect woman included only physical and other superficial qualities. Since communication and friendship were not part of his dream, the women he meets whom he can relate to are not interesting to him. He never forgot Sue who was the woman he couldn't have, the one who got away. John unlike some dreamers realized he had a problem, but unfortunately he was powerless to change it.

Ted, thirty-six, was another dreamer. A blonde, blue-eyed glamorous virgin was what he was after. Like John, the women he chose didn't want him and the ones who liked him were not appealing to him. Fast cars, boats, money and sexy women were his passions. Holding to his dream of meeting a virgin, upon discovering that each woman had what he called "skeletons in her closet, " he would reject her. Ted's goals were to marry and have children. Every year he became older and time passed without his being able to achieve his goals. Helplessness and hopelessness are the plight of dreamers.

I introduced Ted to Debbie, an attractive but not sexy thirty-five year old who also wanted marriage and a family. They went out on a date where she behaved very seductively and ended up going to bed. Later, she informed him she was pregnant. He helped her to obtain an abortion.

If Ted had not held on to his dream of a sexy virgin, his relationship with Debbie may have been the answer to both of their prayers. Sometimes what we want is right in front of us, if we could only release the fantasy.

Walter was an example of a seeker. A tall, retired Croatian gentleman, he came to one of my information nights on the advice of my assistant. Arriving late, he sat at the front in the only available seat, where I had direct eye contact with him. As I spoke, I noticed how gentle he looked as he listened intently to my words. With how much understanding, I did not know at the time.

A few days later, to my surprise, he called to make an appointment to join. I heard his story, as I did everyone's. He was awaiting a divorce from a manipulative woman, who had been unfaithful to him. He was recovering from the loneliness after the break up of a brief relationship, which he knew was wrong for him.

In his efforts to define his preferences, Walter appeared very vague and general but I was later to discover he was quite specific. The only real stipulation he had was that the woman be free to travel. Most everything else he left up to me. Then he informed me he was moving and requested that I put his file on hold. "Freeze me!" he had said.

Not wishing to introduce such a sensitive man to some of the aggressive, controlling women I had on file in his age group, I started asking around to some of the nicer women I had as clients to see if they had any friends who might be interested in Walter. None of these women materialized because Walter was still frozen and unmatched when I had my next information night about six weeks later.

At that seminar, a woman appeared who I felt may be right for Walter. I had to convince her to join as she had many apprehensions, which were fed in part by her over protective daughters. Telling her about Walter helped her to come aboard. Her name was Anne and she was a tall fair-haired dignified English woman in her middle fifties, the widow of a physician.

After she joined, I described her to Walter in terms of her looks and character. He asked me three questions. How tall was she? What color was her hair? Did she work full time? I told him she was a woman of high moral standards and had a sense of humor. It all seemed to meet with his approval and he agreed to call her. Excitedly, I awaited the results. Walter had invited her to dinner at his apartment for their first date and everything had gone well. It was then that he told me he had visualized the right woman for him about six months earlier. His vision was of a tall woman about five feet eight, with fair or gray hair, loyal and faithful. When he opened the door to his apartment on the first night he found exactly what he had envisioned-except he had not given her a face. He found she was acceptable in every way.

Anne must have found him acceptable as they were married a year later. They now spend many months of the year on an island in the Adriatic, since he is retired and she is able to take considerable time off from her job.

Later, I questioned Walter about his visualizations. He told me he imagined an empty picture on the wall. In it he placed whatever he wanted and concentrated on it. This procedure worked one time when he needed one thousand dollars. He visualized the money in the frame and concentrated on it until his head ached. The money came to him within a few hours from a perfectly normal source, but his headache continued for twenty-four hours.

Another time he was looking for an apartment. He visualized one bedroom plus as he wanted to have room for a study. Later, he found a one-bedroom apartment that he liked and returned to his old apartment to give notice. After doing so he went back to sign the lease, when the manager remembered he had one other suite available. There it was - one bedroom with a small foyer near the entrance, which could be used as a study.

After their marriage, Walter used his creative visualization ability to find the right apartment for himself and Anne.

I am sure Walter's ability will continue. I started telling his story in my information nights to show the difference between seeking and dreaming.

Change is difficult. There was one client who appeared to make the transition from a dreamer to a seeker. A young Italian name Gino told me he spend two hours a day, day dreaming about his perfect mate. When he realized I disapproved, he said, "It doesn't hurt anyone."

"It only hurts you," I replied, "It is preventing you from having a relationship."

About two months later he found a woman who was compatible. They moved in together and were making plans to marry. I feel confident he took my advice.

I am not able to prove it, but am convinced that dreamers end up dreaming until their dying day, while seekers find what they want. Which do you want to be?

Chapter 12 Definitions

Over the years of working with single men and women, I came to realize that there were types of singles. In this chapter, I have tried to categorize them as closely as one can when dealing with human beings. I have come up with eight categories, although there may be some overlapping. For example, one person may fit into more than one category. As singleness is sometimes seen as a disease by both singles and society at large, some of these definitions are medical in origin.

1. The Chronically Single. This includes those whose singleness expands a long period of time, probably years or even decades, with intermittent and short periods of being coupled. They are constantly looking for a relationship and usually go from one brief encounter to another with nothing ever developing into long term.

2. The Terminally Single. These are the chronically single who have not accepted it as a way of life and are destined to die of it. They view singleness as somehow incorrect and are probably going to die of the struggle to correct it.

3. The Acutely Single. These are the people who have spent the greater part of their lives in a long-term relationship but through death or divorce have found themselves single. Their singleness is not through choice but rather through circumstance. Being victims

of it, they are usually in a great deal of pain and grief, which they feel, can only be relieved by another relationship. Consequently they are desperate to be coupled again.

4. The Successfully Single. This category includes those who have accepted singleness as a way of life, cope well and take advantage of the state in all its forms. These are well-adjusted people who date others and are open to a relationship if they could only fit it into their busy schedule.

5. The Born Again Single. These are newly single either by choice or mutual agreement with a partner. They are excited about their new state and are characterized by a "starry eyed" appearance. In a chronic state of euphoria, they are naively and adventurously seeking to "meet people."Almost everyone they come in contact with is a potential lover and they are fascinated by the whole singles' scene. Reliving their lost teens these born agains find this state temporary when suddenly reality hits them and they are seriously wounded or they again become coupled.

6. The Confirmed Single. They are similar to the successfully single with the exception that they are closed to the idea of a relationship. They go through periodic and short-lived impulses to be coupled but this is usually temporary. When it comes to actually meeting someone, they back off. The truth is they have set such firm boundaries that no one would dare intrude upon them and their thinking is so rigid that they are closed to anything new in their lives.

7. The Consciously Single This group is made up of a few rare people who have taken the time between relationships to heal and have accepted responsibility for their failures. Often they have done some research, counselling and introspection in the field of relationships and are determined to make changes within themselves. They usually know what they want, keeping a watchful eye out for potential problems The problem with being consciously single is that they find

they are too mature for the other seven categories and consequently find it difficult to establish relationships.

8. The Raging Single. On the surface this group appears to be normal but under a cool exterior is an angry child, seething because of parental or spousal abuse or both. Women particularly are desperately seeking a man but the underlying emotion is hate. They are out to punish every man for what has been done to them. Once in a relationship, they revert to all forms of game playing, manipulation and control. Of course a willing partner is necessary and the end result, if any partner stays around long enough, is a power struggle. These types of relationships can be short lived or can last over a period of time depending on how long each person is willing to participate. Raging singles usually have the same type of relationships throughout their lives only with different partners.

The unfortunate thing about all of the above is that none of them is likely to be successful in getting into a healthy relationship or perhaps any relationship at all. There are exceptions of course and for these I make a ninth category. I call them the Fools because like the fool in the Tarot deck, they take a risk and in their innocence they succeed because they lack the wisdom to fear failure. Defying all laws these are the wonderful people who make a matchmaker's work worthwhile.

Chapter 13   Gracefully Surrendering

My belief is that during our three score and ten years on this planet, we pass through various normal and natural phases, each with its own joys and sorrows. From my own experience, I went through a grieving time when I grieved my lost youth Before I could move on to the next stage, I had to accept the grief and accept what it had to offer. To me happiness is to be found in experiencing loss, grieving and then moving on.

During my five years at the agency, I frequently encountered men and women who were in complete denial about who they were, particularly, their age. What I found with many of my clients was that they were unwilling and refusing to accept the change trying to deceive themselves and the world that they were still young. Many were trying to find the fountain of youth on the jogging trail, hiking trail, climbing or skiing, working out so they could avoid the fact that time had passed. Women had their faces lifted, their chins and tummies tucked and their bodies mutilated by plastic surgeons in an attempt to remain forever young.

I heard from both men and women the declaration that chronologically, "I'm fifty eight, but I am fit as anyone of thirty. My body has no extra fat and I don't enjoy people my own age. They are too old for me."

It is my opinion that these people are neither here nor there. Too vain to allow themselves the growth experience of mid life crisis, they are denying themselves the opportunity of experiencing a rebirth, a new beginning which can only come with letting go of the past. I am not suggesting that they should stop being active and let themselves fall into a state of sedentary deterioration. Instead they should accept aging as a necessary and wonderful part of being human. Their own peer groups often see these people as shallow, and in the age group they are emulating, they are seen as being in their second childhood or boogying with the jet set. They find they belong nowhere. Being hurt jilted or passed by seems to be their fate.

A sixty-two year old "fitness nut" tall, skinny, bald and extremely wrinkled refused to meet any woman who had the least bit of fat on her body. He bragged that he only associated with people his thirty year-old daughter's age. Consequently, two women around the age of fifty rejected him, because they claimed he looked as though he was in his seventies.

Another fifty-year-old man was introduced to a thirty-six year old model type woman. She found him stuffy, boring and inhibited. He was certain that if I had told her he was only forty-two, she would have been interested in him.

Why are so many people not willing to gracefully surrender the things of youth? My guess is it is partly social and partly INSTINCT! The year is 1996. Man reached the moon a quarter of a century ago. Technology has infiltrated every aspect of life. Pushing buttons miles from the battlefield can fight wars. And yet as the third millennium approaches, with almost foolproof birth control, and fertilization outside the womb, people are till slaves to their instincts.

What do I mean by instincts? I am talking about mating. In the animal world as in the world of primitive man, mating occurs spontaneously. The male without thought, seeks any female who is receptive, the only prerequisite if that she be ripe for it. He must compete with other virile males to be the victor. The stronger he is physically, the better are his chances. The female accepts the victor as her mate and the father of her unborn. She then goes off to give birth and to nurture her newly born offspring. The male then moves on to another ripe female.

There appears to be little difference between this physical act of copulation and what goes on today with modern human kind. The most desirable women are the ones who are young, of childbearing age and beautiful. A young, slender, gorgeous, healthy woman, an ovum begging for the right sperm, she finds she has countless suitors and many choices.

Who is the best candidate to meet her requirements as a sperm donor? Why a healthy, strong, attractive male who has the capacity to gather much food and to protect the vulnerable female and her young from predators. In other words, he must be tall virile, aggressive, successful, most likely a professional with a huge income and endless financial potential.

That means that anyone who does not fit with the above description is not considered desirable, Women who are past menopause, are not attractive or are overweight have the most difficulty finding partners. Men who are short, small, overweight, tradesmen, labourers, and men in low paying, unprestigious jobs are in the same boat as the older unattractive females. Younger males and females who were either infertile or choose not to have children were also very difficult to match. A beautiful young woman could have almost any man she chose. Likewise a man with enough bucks could have any woman. Since people of all ages came to the agency, there was always the problem of having an abundance of women over forty-five and an abundance of men under forty who were unskilled or with low incomes.

Many of the older women had been left by a man who found a younger woman. Some had been widowed or left an abusive situation. After a lengthy marriage, most of these women were seeking men who were equal in income or status to their former spouse, not realizing that they themselves had slipped from the most desirable to the most undesirable group of women. They would find that men in their own age group were not interested in them but in younger more attractive women. This would leave the middle aged woman with few possibilities, either men older than themselves and men less successful and wealthy than their husbands or younger men who were insecure and needing to be mothered or remaining alone.

The young unsuccessful, low prestige low-income male found that older better-established professional men were snapping up most of the attractive women. These less desirable and often nice men found they had to settle for a woman who was not beautiful and perhaps overweight.

Everything isn't simple for those who can choose either. The young beautiful woman may be faced with struggling to maintain her beauty and youthful appearance so her husband doesn't leave her for someone younger and more beautiful, when she is forty-five and has raised his children. The older successful man with the beautiful young chick may find himself competing heavily with younger more virile males to keep the attention of his prize. Once he has landed his prize he may find he must fight to defend it. This may include having a second family against his will or living a lifestyle, which is too fast for his advancing years. The consequence of such a match may include blows to his self-esteem, or losing his wealth to the extravagant living of his young bride. The final blow to his peace of mind may come when he reaches retirement age when he finds he must keep struggling to pay orthodontic bills for his children and future college expenses. He also has the worry of his bride disappearing if he suddenly finds himself penniless.

Matchmaking for the over fifties becomes an impossible dream. Men of that age refuse to meet fifty-year-old women and are demanding thirty-five year olds. The women are refusing to meet men in their sixties and are wanting forty year olds with money who in turn are looking for twenty-five to thirty year olds. Everyone is driven by their instincts and the situation appears out of control.

There did appear to be a coming to the senses for which I was greatly relieved, when men approached retirement. With a change in lifestyle looming on the horizon, many men were able to take a more practical approach to their choice of mate. Then having someone who was at the same place in life as he, with freedom to travel and pursue creative endeavours becomes a priority, rather than having a gorgeous young thing on his arm to impress his colleagues. Matching the retirement age group proved to be somewhat more rewarding due to this change in perspective.

After making all these observations and conclusions about the whole issue of age, beauty, instincts, what can I advise the seekers as they enter the meet market? I do believe there are alternatives to being rejected on the basis of your looks, age or income or rejecting others on that basis. There were clients who were able to overcome their instincts and gracefully surrender and in doing so found happiness, I believe that answer is to found in making a choice to become conscious.

Becoming conscious means examining closely one's priorities in life and in possibly changing one's perspective in order to find joy. This is done first, by knowing who you are and what you want. The following questions may be asked, first of all of older women. Is a man's financial worth all that important to a woman who has her own financial independence and is past childbearing age? Perhaps a good man is more important than a rich one. Certainly, no woman wants to support her man but how important is it that he matches her dollar for dollar? Secondly, we all change in time. How important is it that he be physically attractive? Perhaps someone with similar goals, values and interests would be more valuable. Thirdly, does age really matter? Emotional maturity is more important.

To the men I would ask is it that important that the woman stimulate you sexually, now that you are past procreation? We all know that passion and physical chemistry diminish in time. I see men compromise emotional maturity for great sex. The price they pay in the long run is horrendous. Is a woman's age that important? Is impressing other men that important? Perhaps what you really want is a woman who understands you and shares your hopes and dreams.

For both men and women, especially those in their middle years, I would urge you to gracefully surrender the things of youth. I urge you to move on to a fuller, richer life where your choices and decisions are based on self-acceptance and your goals for the second half of your life. Gracefully surrendering means letting go of functioning from your instincts only and making conscious choices from a deeper part of yourself. From there you can choose your mate regardless of age, looks, wealth and position and perhaps have some joy in your life.

Chapter 14   I Have Heard it All, Now!

During the years in the introduction business, I had a number of unusual requests, particularly over the telephone when people called for information. That was when I screened clients. It was very easy to tell which ones were crank calls or requests, which were beyond the limits of the agency.

Physical qualities especially female anatomy, was an area which leant itself to specifics. By far the majority of men were looking for slim, fit women but occasionally I would receive a request for a full-bodied woman or a woman up to twenty pounds overweight. One call, which I felt to be a crank call, was from a man who wanted to meet a woman a hundred pounds overweight and who had cellulite. Since I discouraged the extremely overweight, I told the man I couldn't help him.

Breasts were an area of concern to the men. Many requested a woman with large ones, but one man preferred women who were flat chested. One undiplomatic client asked of his match, on the first phone call, "Are you shapely?" Needless to say, she refused to meet him at all. Another man who spoke of women like they were livestock, asked me for a specific woman's measurements. I informed him we didn't record that type of information.

Only once did male anatomy come up as a preference. A forty-year-old woman requesting an uncircumcised male, wanted to write it on her profile for everyone to read. I assured her that it would appear too threatening for most men and would likely be a turnoff. I told her she would have to find out that type of information for herself, as I didn't record it. She ended up in a relationship with the first man she met, so I assumed that he met with her approval in that area.

Some clients had very unrealistic ideas about what I could do for them. One man in his early forties, divorced with a teenage daughter, was certain he didn't want more children. Refusing to meet women his own age, because they weren't attractive enough, he demanded twenty and thirty year olds. When I explained that women of that age group wanted children, he told me I should be offering seminars to reprogram the women into not wanting children. I told him I could no more do that than I could reprogram the men into not wanting younger, attractive women.

On one occasion a very handsome young man, dark haired with a beautiful tan dropped by the office to offer his services. He explained that he couldn't pay but was willing to help me out. I discovered he was unemployed, unskilled and new to the city. He looked quite dejected when I told him the women I had were looking for marriage and families and he would need more to offer than a beautiful body. During my years at the agency, I had more than one visitor to Canada or alien from a foreign country wanting to marry a Canadian woman so he could stay in the country. I could just imagine presenting such a man to one of my high profile, successful female lawyers!

Fortunately, I did not receive too many obscene phone calls or have many embarrassing situations. One call came close to obscene was from a young man wondering if I had any older women who might be willing to help him with his sexual frustrations. I assured him I didn't. One embarrassing situation occurred in one of my information nights, when a man announced he was bisexual, had a male partner already but wanted to meet some women as well. Luckily, this was the only such incident during my seminars.

In the beginning, I received a lot of calls from men who mistakenly thought it was an escort service. These calls came in at night, on the answering machine or voice mail. Mostly they were from men who were out of town, staying at hotels. In time I came to recognize them as escort service calls. If I spoke directly to the men, I would explain to them that it was not an escort service. Some would apologize and hang up. Others would pretend that they had called about a relationship, book an appointment and then not show up. I learned to take such calls and appointments as a joke.

I had three men over the years, which dropped in to see me, wanting to join the service and pretended they were interested in renting an office in the building. They had each forgotten their money, made appointments to join and then didn't show. One of them was posing as a plastic surgeon at a local hospital. When he didn't keep his appointment, I called the hospital and discovered he was unknown there. I came to be very suspicious of anyone looking for office space.

Sometimes people who were married or in relationships would call me and ask if I thought joining and meeting someone new would help them to get out of a bad situation. Other times, I would receive messages to call someone. When I returned the call, I would ask for that person. The person on the other end of the line would say yes it was they, but when I told them who I was, they would swear up and down they had not called me. Probably, they were in a relationship and their partner was within hearing distance of the call. Or they didn't want anyone to know they had called an introduction service.

The days spent in the office of such a service never ceased to be interesting and provided material for conversation and laughter. I came to view human nature with a renewed tolerance and understanding.

Chapter 15   What Is Love?

Throughout the ages, poets, playwrights, philosophers and theologians have attempted to define love. The truth is no one really knows the complexity of love or the extent of its power. To define it in a sentence or paragraph is impossible since it is so complex and yet so simple that language, which is limited to our human understanding, cannot explain it. It is rather like God, in that it is so limitless that to try to define it is to limit it. The truth is that love exists in many forms and has many purposes so we must carefully regard which type of love we are meaning.

We all, regardless of age, race, color or creed desire to love and be loved. Love can only be expressed through our relationships with others. Why is it that something we seek so desperately and feels so good to us at one time can be totally devastating and destructive to us at other times? Since none of us is alone in the world, we are forced into having relationships with others. The truth is we cannot live without relationships and often we cannot live with them because they hurt so much. Love seems to be the source of our greatest joy and our greatest pain. Is that love?

Let's look at the purposes of relationships. Why do we have them? The first reason is instinctive. That is survival. We have relationships because there is strength in numbers. We have a better chance of surviving if there are two or more of us together facing the odds. Our chances of survival increase if we are a couple or a family or a community, a tribe and we attain the maximum strength if we are part of a nation.

The second reason for having relationships is also instinctive. It is procreation. Procreation insures that the species, the race carries on. Not all relationships are procreative, but those, which are not often, take on the flip side of procreation, which is co-creation.

Co-creation means that people have come together for the purpose of building something. Business partnerships, community, church and government are examples of co-creation. Sexual relationships can be co-creative if the two partners have a mutual goal to build or create something.

A fourth reason people have relationships if for pleasure. This can take the form of fun, sharing experiences, sex and the joy a loving experience can give us. Since we are social beings, we find life can be more pleasurable if we can live it with a fellow being.

Philosophers and metaphysicians tell us there is a fifth reason for relationships. This is one we do not readily seek and may try at all cost to avoid, but nevertheless benefit from in the long run. That purpose is growth and healing. We can learn from our interaction with others and we can often heal old issues and thus mature into a deeper and stronger person because of having had a particular relationship. This is the type of relationship I had with my late husband. In the beginning I believed it was for pleasure and co-creation but now I know its purpose was healing. I am grateful for having had it in spite of all the pain it brought at the time.

Next I intend to try to define love in its various forms as I came to understand it. The following diagram will assist in the explanations. Love exists in four separate but often overlapping forms, each with its own purpose. The first is instinctive love. This is included in part in what the Greeks called Erotic love or familial love. The second type of love is Emotional love or what the Greeks also called Erotic love. The third is intellectual love or Filial love using the Greek term. The fourth type is Divine love or as the Greeks termed it Agape. I will describe each in detail.

Physical Love. Physical love occurs at the level of the body and for that reason it can be called instinctive. It is an innate, unconscious powerful drive. It is a conditional love, the conditions being physical. It is reactive, meaning the being responds or reacts to a physical stimulus. The most obvious example of this is the sex drive, which is pleasure seeking. It involves physical attraction to another body and all the terms we use to describe it such as hormones, chemistry and love at first sight. Also instinctive is the familial side, which is the love of parents for children. It is unconscious, innate and involuntary. Mothers are driven to nurture and protect their young both in the animal and human world. The purpose of this love is simply, the survival of the species. Instinctive love exists only in the present and once its purpose is complete, either mating or raising young, it is finished. At the human level it could be exemplified by a one-night stand or a mother dashing in front of an oncoming car to protect her child, where procreation or survival is the unconscious goal. Sexual relationships, which are merely physical, are short lived unless the couple can have one or more of the next types of love in their relationship.

Emotional Love. This type of love has to do with the heart, the feelings and emotions. Also known as erotic love or romantic love, it is pleasure seeking but the pleasure sought is an emotional high or heightened sensation of the emotions. Many of these emotions are learned from others or the media. It is often described as falling in love, passion, fatal attraction and infatuation. It is highly motivating as the definition of emotion is "moving out." It manifests itself in such feelings as excitement elation, ecstasy, reckless abandonment and obsession. Emotional love is conditional, the conditions being what we call positive emotions. For example, "I love you if you keep exciting me." Emotional love is by and large learned although it is also instinctive. It is reactive since the person is constantly reacting with his emotions to what his partner is doing. There is always a deep attachment to the other and that attachment can easily be transferred to another should the first love object be unavailable. The positive thing about emotional love is that it is exciting and interesting to those involved.

On the negative side, it is not possible for it to remain positive because positive is always balanced by negative. Emotions go up and down like a roller coaster. The more intensely exciting a relationship is the more intensely negative and painful it is destined to be. The following are some of the negative feelings of an erotic relationship. Fear is the most prevalent, fear of loss, and fear of abandonment by the partner. Other feelings are anxiety, jealousy, envy, hate, rejection, repulsion, bondage, guilt, insecurity, helplessness, disappointment, anger, depression, being used and abused, worthlessness. Power struggles, manipulation, emotional blackmail and mind games are some of the activities carried on by the participants. Emotional relationships usually derive the most pleasure from memories of the past or fantasies about the future. When the longed for partner finally arrives on the scene there is usually a lot of emotion such as disappointment over it not being the way it was imagined.

Is this love? It doesn't sound like it. M. Scott Peck describes love as "the will to extends one's self for the purpose of nurturing one's own or another's spiritual growth. It is an extension of one's ego boundaries to include another."5 Of falling in love he states that it is not an act of will, an extension of one's boundaries but a temporary lapse of them and is definitely not for the purpose of nurturing spiritual growth. In fact Peck goes on to say that is a trick our genes play on us to trap us into procreation. Falling in love is always followed by falling out of love.

Where does this leave living happily ever after? It is not to be found in emotional love. Staying in that starry eyed state would be like trying to remain drunk permanently. Drunkenness is eventually followed by unconsciousness, sickness or a hangover. There are three possible outcomes to falling in love. One, it can simply die. Two, it becomes an addiction, where one feels he cannot live without it and it will destroy his self esteem and all other creative aspects of his life. Three, it can evolve into a higher and more expansive love, intellectual love or the highest form of love which is unconditional love. For this to happen, it will take a conscious effort on the part of the participants.

If emotional love is so volatile, what is its purpose? Its purpose is procreation and commitment. Like instinctive love, it brings people together for having babies but carries it one step further. The positive emotions keep people together and so do the negative emotions. Women stay with their husbands out of fear, fear of being alone and unable to provide for children. Husbands stay with wives out of guilt. These are only examples and not typical of every situation. Emotions are what keep relationships together so the helpless are cared for and everyone benefits from it. The only problem is that there may be little room for self-expression and creativity in such arrangement. Participants often put up with abuse, feel bound and worthless because they are unable to free themselves of the negativity of the situation.

Intellectual Love. Some fortunate people are able to relate to their partner in another way as well as through the emotions and consequently experience the glue which may hold the relationship together in a more fulfilling and enjoyable way. Termed Filial love by the Greeks, intellectual love is the love of friends. It involves the meeting of the minds and occurs at the level of ideas, of thinking or discerning or the will. It involves choices based on logic rather than feelings. It requires some common ground between the two friends, some understanding and similarities. It seeks mutual benefit, agreement and validation. While experiencing intellectual love, friends can share ideas, can create together and have healthy boundaries and standards in place. Relating as friends is by and large learned from family, and media and others. It is a conditional form of love in that it contingent upon choices and the choice to agree or disagree or agree to disagree.

Although a more conscious type of love than emotional and physical love, it does have disadvantages and limitations. One of these is that our judgment comes into play and we are constantly evaluating everything in dualities. Our intellect sees everything as right or wrong, good or bad, black or white. There is little room for unconditional acceptance. The intellect can be controlling since it likes to be right. Friendships sometimes lack the excitement of the emotions and can be rather dry or even boring at times. However, friends have the option of exercising choice and can be active or proactive in the relationship rather than reactive. Intellectual relationships function in the present and are not based on memories of the past or fantasies about the future. How can friendships add a higher dimension to a relationship? Firstly they allow the participants the right to choose rather than being swept into a relationship by some outside force such as passion and being held there by fear or some other negative emotion. Secondly they allow opportunity for the growth and creativity of those involved. If a couple can add friendship to passion and procreation, they are much more likely to experience a normal, healthy relationship.

Divine Love-Agape or unconditional love is something we rarely experience at the human level or if we do, it is seen in passing glimpses and fleeting moments. Meaning the love of God, it is the kind of love St. Paul spoke of when he said, "Love is patient, love is kind. It does not envy, it does not boast, it is not proud, it is not easily angered, it keeps no record of wrong. Love does not delight in evil but rejoices with the truth, always hopes, always perseveres. Love never fails."6 Shakespeare speaks of the unchanging aspect of love when he states that, "Love is not love which alters when if alteration finds or bends with the remover to remove."7 Unconditional love is love given with no thought of return. It carries no judgment and there are no conditions attached to it. If I am truly experiencing unconditional love, then I cannot stop loving someone when they are doing something I feel is wrong. I cannot be unloved if what I do does not please them. Divine love is eternal, unlimited, unchanging, constant. There are no expectations and no judgements with Divine Love. There is no passion, therefore no pain. The best way I can describe it is that it is neutral, neither exciting nor having any emotion. It is a complete unconditional acceptance of our loved one just as they are regardless of their actions. It is the way God loves us. Some feel that parents' love for children is unconditional. It is only if they hold no expectations of the child or judgement about the actions of the child. The closest I have ever come to unconditional love is with my cat. I never stop loving her even when she breaks my favourite ornament or wakes me up at six a.m. on my day off. I know she is just a cat and I have no unrealistic expectations of her. Therefore she never disappoints me. If I could only have that kind of relationship with another human being! Unfortunately my intellect, judgement or emotions always seem to get in the way. This is the problem with being human. Because we live in a conditional world, it would be detrimental to have unconditional love for everyone. We would end up being a doormat and victim to every kind of exploitation known to man. We must use our feelings to gauge whether there is something wrong and our intellect to make choices about the merits of the relationship.

Divine love is about charity not about being used. Divine love means loving oneself enough to say no to a relationship that is wrong for us even though we may love that person deeply. Divine love is about loving ourselves enough to have boundaries and standards. Divine love means allowing another to be free to do what he or she feels is right regardless of whether we approve or agree. Divine love may mean saying good-bye to a person or relationship that is not for our highest good, without ending our love for that person. We can release that person because we love them and ourselves.

Divine love in its true state is healing, creative, mature and empowering. I believe it is innate in all of us but unconscious. We know and recognize its greatness once we have been touched by it. I believe it is neither learned nor instinctive. Instead it is remembered from that part of ourselves which has been forgotten by the complex process of living. That part is our higher self.

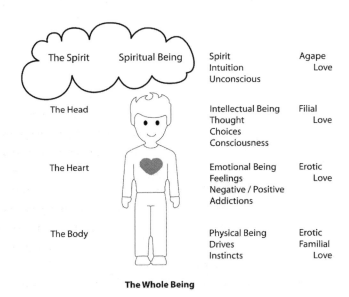

The Whole Being

5.pp 81
6 I Corinthians, Chapter 13 Verses 4-8
7. Shakespeare, William, Sonnet CXVI

Chapter 16   What Is Love?   Part II

When we presented the material in the previous chapter, my husband and I found it was not always met with enthusiasm. It was not what most people wanted to hear. Most of them wanted to hear that highly erotic relationships are available to everyone and that they can last forever. Of course, these were the people who related through their emotions and consequently were having the most difficulty finding a satisfactory relationship. Much of the material taught was my husband's. We tried to convince them that before someone can have a healthy partnership he must be willing to accept the truth about erotic love and also must be willing to have something more stable and mature.

We attempted to teach the following concepts. To understand the various types of love, we need to know where each is coming from. Our physical body, emotions, mind and higher self are a part of the whole being, which is united for our highest good. Each of the parts must function in harmony with the other and is not separate from any of the others. The following diagram of a cart with a driver pulled by a horse provides a concrete metaphor of the whole human being. The cart represents the body, the vehicle for mind, emotions and spirit. The horse is the emotions, which provide energy or fuel for the vehicle to move ahead. The driver is the intellect or the thinking mind, which gives verbal instructions to the horse. Behind the driver is the master or spirit who we may be unaware of. Let us look at each in detail.

The cart or the body has little control of its own. As a cart, it will respond to the horse that responds to the driver. The body too, responds to the stimuli and experiences such sensations as pleasure and pain. To give the body or the cart complete control means more than to deny the higher parts of ourselves namely the emotions, intellect or spirit, and to functions as an animal reacting to physical stimuli. At this level all activity would be directed toward survival, pleasure seeking or pain avoidance.

To give the emotions control, would be to allow such feeling as excitement, fear, anger to control us as a runaway horse would control a cart and driver. At times I have had dreams about being in a vehicle drawn by a horse and having the horse not only running away but turning to attach the cart and occupants. This dream tells me that my emotions are out of control and are having a destructive effect on my health, my mind and my spirit.

Intellectuals believe the mind to be the highest part of ourselves, but I do not believe that. Giving control to the mind or the driver may mean we are limiting ourselves to our thoughts and therefore limiting our potential. As the driver can only direct the horse to destinations he has been or understands or analyzed, so the rational mind can only lead us to what we have already done or to what seems reasonable or logical.

Many of us go through life seeking physical stimuli. Others allow sensations and fears to run their lives. Still others devote their lives to analyzing and over analyzing every challenge. Most do not realize that behind their thoughts, instinct and emotions is the master who is quietly waiting for us to seek direction from it. This silent being, who is behind everything, holds the key to more conscious living, to really being in control of our lives, which is to stop controlling and surrender. To surrender is to open up to growth and learn and have experiences we have never had. This master can lead us to self-mastery if we decide to turn the cart, horse and driver over to him. What happens if we choose to let the master be in charge? This does not mean we ignore our bodies, minds and emotions. It means we use them for the purpose for which they we intended. To give control to one or all of them is so be out of control. To deny them means to deny our humanity. Instead of giving control to or denying these three parts of being human, we can use them as a means of discovering our own higher self.

How can the body teach us? Animals use their bodies to guide them. They know when they are in danger. They know when it is time to mate. They know when they are going to die. We also know these things innately but have learned to tune them out. The body gives us messages. It tells us if something feels good and it tells us if something is wrong, when we feel pain, fatigue or sickness. Our instincts also speak to us through our intuition, if we will listen. It can appear as a sense of discomfort or foreboding. If a relationship is giving us bodily or intuitive discomfort, then it is obviously causing us stress and needs to be examined. These messages are then conveyed to the mind or the driver, who can use the information to make a decision.

How can the emotions help us to become more conscious? We hear a lot about "getting into our feelings" Many people misinterpret this to mean we should be seeking emotional highs as our goal in life. I feel this is a misuse of emotion since it serves to bring us nothing but misery. Instead "getting into our feelings" means we need to examine what we are feeling and name the emotion. Positive emotions such as excitement can motivate us to be creative and carry out the ideas provided to us by the intellect. Negative emotions such as fear or jealousy can serve to tell us there is something wrong. Our mind can then question why and to make a decision based on the answer. This happens the same way the horse can send messages to the driver that danger is impending. The intellect can them make a rational choice about the direction to take. Emotions by themselves are destructive but if used as a means to an end, they can serve as a valuable tool in life.

How does the intellect function to help us grow into self-mastery? It is there to receive and evaluate data provided by the instinct, and the emotions to make rational decisions. Let me give an example. I had a male client in his forties, a lawyer who was very intellectual. He desperately wanted to marry and have children. After meeting a thirty-nine year old woman, whom he found very compatible, he did some research on their chances of conceiving a child. He read that a couple of their age had only a fifty percent chance of conceiving. He immediately broke off the relationship with the idea of finding a younger woman. Three years later he was still searching. This man had let his mind or driver take control. He made a rational choice based on data he had gathered. However he failed to listen to his heart and his intuition that told him that everything was all right. He had also failed to surrender to his master. By overanalyzing, he put his mind in complete control and destroyed any chance of allowing something greater to take over. Decisions based on intellect are good but sometimes miracles are better if we are prepared to let something larger than ourselves work on our behalf.

It is not my desire to downplay or discredit any of the four types of love. I am only saying that if a relationship is to exist over time, it needs elements of all four.

Let us imagine that a relationship has all of these. That does not mean that issues will r arise which cause confrontations. John Bradshaw in his book, Homecoming 8, he states that in a healthy relationship, issues can be confronted. Issues can be confronted!

If they cannot, then those involved will likely have a sense of foreboding and a negative emotion that may feel like hopelessness.

If issues can and must be confronted, in a healthy relationship, then how is this done. First we need to identify the emotions and intuitive feeling and decide with our intellect just what is happening that we don't like and why. We may also need to decide what we like. Then we need to define what we would like to have happen. What outcome do we want?

This means taking some time to reflect. Then I would recommend writing it down in the affirmative. In a healthy relationship, people need to set aside time to talk constructively. It is not possible to do justice to a healthy confrontation when one is dashing out the front door to work in the morning. The subject needs to be approached in honesty and forthrightness. It also needs to be addressed from the first person, singular. Instead of saying, "You are doing this, this and this which makes me mad," we need to say, "It really upsets me when you do this. I feel _____when you do this." Our partner has as much invested in the relationship as we do, then he cannot help but listen. We need to listen to what our partner has to say as well, since she may have as many issues to confront as we do.

What are the possible outcomes of such a confrontation? There are two. The first is that we come to realize that we have unrealistic expectations of the other and we need to let go of these expectations. Or there may be the realization that one needs to encompass a greater acceptance of the other and oneself. Thus we discover that the relationship if okay and that expressing our honest feelings was beneficial in bringing us closer. The other outcome is that we decide that the relationship is not okay and that we have compromised ourselves and our values to keep peace. We may realize we have become a co-conspirator or an accomplice to something that is unacceptable to us. The only answer is to release the relationship if we want to maintain our self-respect.

Either of the above alternatives means that unconditional love is being expressed. Boundaries are being set and both partners are free to be themselves. This is true love.

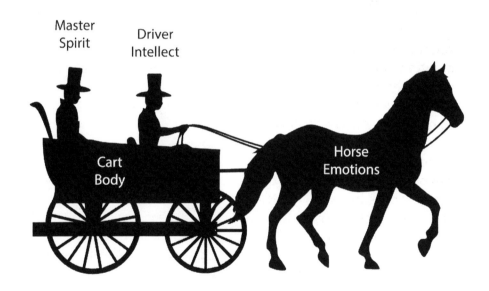

Whole Being

8. Bradshaw, John, Homecoming, Bantam Books, N. Y. 1990

Chapter 17   The Lawsuit

One of the most devastating events in the history of my life as a matchmaker was the time I was sued by a client. It happened during my first year when I had the least experience, the least confidence and the least resilience. I remember a few months earlier I was watching a television interview with a woman who owned a huge introduction service in the United States. She was giving some information about the magnitude of her service, the number of clients she had, the exorbitant fees she was charging and the fact that she had several law suits pending against her at the time of the interview. I remember thinking how grateful I was it wasn't happening to me. It also made me realize that lawsuits are part of that type of business.

Among the clients that I had taken over from my predecessor, was a woman of approximately sixty years who had joined the previous summer. My husband had spoken with her when she had come in to introduce herself. That week he was finishing off his church and a weekend retreat was being held, during which his successor was to take over. During his conversation with Madeline, he told her about the retreat and she signed up for it.

Thinking that she was interested in the retreat and had no hidden agendas, I met her at the first session. She was very friendly to me, telling me how much she wanted to meet someone. She said she didn't like men her age, but would like to meet a man in his early fifties. Attempting to be realistic with her, I told her that the problem with men in their fifties was that they were usually looking for women in their thirties and forties, but I assured her I would do my best. She proceeded to tell me that the one man she had met with the previous owner, she liked very much but he didn't want to make a commitment and he had hurt her very much. I expressed my regrets and the conversation ended.

Throughout the retreat, she kept expressing her desire for a relationship, complaining about the accommodations at the retreat and staring at me. The latter, I found quite disconcerting, as her gaze gave me the impression of a puppy dog begging for a bone. I remember thinking there was something sick about those gazes and about the woman who was behind them.

Back at the office that week, she called to say that she had decided to join the church, which was being taken over by my husband's successor. I realized her attendance at the retreat and support of the church was nothing more that an attempt to get on the good side of me.

When she called a few days later, during my first few weeks at the office, she was quite angry and demanding. She wanted to know "just when did I plan to match her?" At that point, I took the time to peruse her file. She worked as a secretary, had less than a high school education, lived in the most prestigious part of the city and was expecting a lot. In her preferences, she had stated, "I am worth half a million dollars and I won't consider anyone who has a penny less!" Also on the form, but crossed out she had said she was French and wanted to meet someone French. I started thinking about what men I had who were in their early fifties, who were very well off and interested in a sixty-year old woman. I came up with zip!

I kept thinking of one man who was French, had studied hotellery in France, was about fifty-one but his job was only a desk clerk in a hotel. He was a pleasant man, wanting a relationship, owned a home in a less prestigious but respectable neighbourhood. Many things seemed to fit except I was not sure of his net worth, but knew his house alone would be worth a couple of hundred thousand.

In an attempt to keep ahead of the matching, in those first few weeks, I went to the office on a Sunday. I telephoned Madeline and asked her if she would meet Rudolph. My intentions were perfectly innocent, but I lived to regret that phone call over the months to come. She agreed to the match and when I called him, he was willing to meet a woman older than himself, I felt pleased with myself for my resourcefulness.

One week later, on a Monday morning, the first call was from Madeline. She was furious about the introduction! They had met and she found Rudolph totally unsuitable. First she claimed I told her he was a hotel owner when he was really a desk clerk. Actually I told her he worked in a hotel. She was very much insulted by his occupation and I didn't know what else. She said he had treated her nicely and taken her out to dinner, where they had a good time. She could not tell me why the introduction was so bad. She then proceeded to tell me how much better the introductions were from the previous owner. She was very angry that I had not mailed her out a copy of the profile as the other owners had done. I reminded her of how one of their introductions had broken her heart. That made her very angry and she said she didn't want to talk to me. I said, "Please call me back when you are in a better mood."

She retorted, "I'll never call you again." And hung up. Mystified I put the phone down. I quickly reviewed in my mind what dreadful deed I had done. I matched her with a younger man as she had requested, he treated her nicely and they enjoyed themselves. He was French as was her background. The only thing I could come up with was that he had a job she felt was beneath her and he wasn't rich. On the other hand she had only a grade ten education and was a secretary. It was that huge house on snob hill, which she had earned through a divorce, which made the difference.

I checked back over the file of the man, Joe, who the previous owner had matched with her. It was sketchy to say the least. His comment about her was that he found her too controlling. This fit my impression of her after my recent telephone conversations. Following these thoughts, I continued with my work.

A few days later, to my surprise, I received a call from my predecessor and many to follow in the next few weeks. Madeline had told mom and dad on me! I was to hear over and over again how upset she was over the ``terrible ``introduction I had given her. Sandi, the previous owner agreed that was not such a bad match. When I questioned her about the man who had broken Madeline's heart, she told me he wasn't really a member. They had taken him on to give some of the women more men to choose from. She also told me he had emotional problems. My husband who knew him slightly confirmed this. The phone calls from Sandi increased as Madeline was passing all messages through her. The calls progressed to threats that if I did not match her soon, she was going to take legal action.

I ignored all these threats, since I knew in my heart that I had done my best. I knew the men I had on file would not meet her requirements as to status and prosperity. Sandi even suggested one gentleman who was in his seventies but he was in a relationship and did not want to meet anyone else. At this point I felt my hands were tied, so I didn't worry about her threats.

I heard from some people in the church that Madeline was questioning them about my integrity, to which they could only give me a positive recommendation. One day I received a copy of a letter she had sent to the Better Business Bureau asking them if either my husband or I had a criminal record. I knew that the BBB responds to formal complaints and then the complainee receives a copy and has a chance to reply and give their side of the story. Her letter didn't follow protocol.

Madeline persisted. I was next to receive a letter from her on her ex-husband's letterhead, asking for a full refund or she would begin litigation. Since I had received none of her fees, which had been paid to the previous owner, I was determined not to fork over a penny. I was still not sure if she was serious about going to court as I had received so many threats from Sandi's clients. They had threatened to sue me. I had come to take them with a grain of salt.

During this time, I had no conversation with Madeline. My husband called her one day just to ask her what she wanted from us. She again expounded on the inappropriateness of her date with Rudolph and how I would not listen to Sandi about how the business should be run. To me it sounded like what she wanted was control.

One day after returning from lunch, I received a telephone message from her marked "urgent." When I called her back she retorted that she didn't want to talk to me but had left a message with the receptionist that she was going to start litigation. Then she hung up the phone with a slam.

I received the writ the next day. It was a summons to appear in small claims court. Madeline was asking for a full refund of her original fee plus court costs. She accused me of not giving her appropriate introductions and of stating that men in their fifties were only interested in women in their twenties and thirties. I couldn't deny any of it and it was only her opinion that Rudolph was inappropriate, I wrote back a counter suit for dues in arrears and damages to my reputation.

Nothing happened for several months but I found out that Madeline had joined another agency. In the meantime my relationship with the previous owners deteriorated due to complaints from their clients, unpaid bills they left behind and the fact that we had closed down a branch in a neighbouring city, which they sold. The proprietor still owed them money and if it was closed they would never get their money. He was another person they had ripped off, sold a dream that was worthless. Sandi had long since stopped calling me to convey threats from Madeline.

Several months later, I received a couriered letter from Sandi, stating that she was appearing as an expert witness at the trial. Also I received a court date, which was earlier that I had expected. By this time I was petrified with fear as nothing like this had ever happened to me before. My husband and I were not communicating at that time and I felt alone and unsupported. Out of fear, I decided to let my lawyer represent me.

My lawyer prepared my case. Since Madeline's contract specified that there were no refunds, we were going to argue that Rudolph was not such a bad match and that I was truthful about her chances. We subpoenaed two of my satisfied clients to testify that the service they received was excellent. Legally it appeared to be cut and dried, but my fears kept niggling away at me.

My lawyer and I arrived at the courthouse at the same time. Madeline was there with no council but instead of Sandi, she brought along Sandi's common law husband who by this time I had come to know as the con artist of all time. Any clients who had dealt with this man had felt totally deceived. It appeared he was to be the "expert witness."

That afternoon, we heard all the cases ahead of ours and when it finally came up, Madeline objected to my lawyer representing me because of the fact that he was a client. The judge then had to take time to consider this before continuing; It was late in the afternoon when he agreed that my lawyer could indeed represent me. Madeline took the stand first, stating how I had forced her to meet Rudolph and when she had complained about the introduction, that I had been very rude to her. When she was questioned as to what I had said, she couldn't remember. A lot of references were made to the retreat that had gone on. The afternoon ended before either of my witnesses or I had a chance to be examined although we were there and ready. The case was delayed until the following afternoon.

The next day my relationship with my husband had improved so he decided to accompany me to court. The afternoon continued, first the other cases were heard and finally ours. This time the con artist got on the stand and testified at great length about the importance of mailing out profiles to clients. He spoke like an authority on the subject even though he had been involved for only a few months. He had actually less experience than I had. I was annoyed that my lawyer didn't pick up on this even though I had briefed him on it. He did not reveal that the con artist was not an expert, had less than grade nine education, little experience and was not even committed enough to actually be married himself. When my lawyer tried to point out that Sandi was still using the company letterhead and that her interest in the case was personal because of the closing of the other office, the judge insisted that it was irrelevant evidence. He was only concerned with the use of profiles, which were not even mentioned in the client contract and were not promised to the client in any binding way.

Everyone said I did well on the stand. I was careful not to say anything derogatory about my predecessors and told the truth from my standpoint. My witnesses also presented themselves well. At the end of the afternoon, my lawyer who came across as a wimp gave a good summation stating that no damages had been done to Madeline and that the agency had acted well on her behalf. The judge, in his wishy-washy way needed time to reflect before making a decision and asked us all to return the next day for the judgement. I did not feel as confident at the end of the day as I did the first day. I kept thinking I should try an out of court settlement and offer Madeline the sum of $350.00. That figure kept crossing my mind.

The next day, my lawyer, my husband and I arrived in court to hear the outcome. There was no evidence of Madeline or her con artist expert witness. When the judge started talking, she was still not there. I kept expecting her to arrive at any moment but she did not. At least I did not have to look at her puppy dogface when the judgement was announced.

The judge made a long speech, which he read, from a piece of paper. He outlined how Madeline, a refined and upper class woman, looking for a marriage partner, had been taken in by an uncaring introduction agency, which was slightly less than honest. He awarded her not the full amount of her fees but the sum of $350.00 plus costs. I had lost. Madeline was not present in her moment of glory. I felt terrible after the outcome, but I tried to put it all behind me. A pervading fear of more law suits kept nibbling away at me but that proved to be the only one I was to experience in my time there.

I decided not to appeal the case. It was just going to cost me more in terms of money and peace of mind. Instead I decided to let go of being a victim. This was a more worthwhile cause for me.

I mailed the cheque for $350.00 plus costs and considered including a note which stated, "You may have won the case, but you'll never have what you want, a man." I didn't. I had grown beyond that. The case cost me a lawyer's fee and a lot of pain.

In time I came to realize that the outcome was in my favour. I got rid of her. She could never come back to my agency and try to control me and mine was the best service in the city. I would never have to try to match her again.

Later I heard from another agency, which Madeline had joined that she wasn't speaking to that owner either and that her best friend was in the process of suing them. I knew I was right about her, that wherever she went she was in conflict. I really pity her.

Chapter 18 Surprises

Over the years at my love business, I discovered most people were predicable in terms of the outcomes of their introductions. Usually they did what they always did and got what they always got. There were however, some people and some couples who surprised me. The twins, the kidney transplant people and the young Italian who gave up daydreaming, were included in this group.

One of the surprises was Peter and Joan. Peter had come to the agency about eighteen months ahead of Joan. His wife had only died about three weeks earlier and was still in the grieving stage when I first met him. He was looking for a woman who could provide the companionship and affection his wife had given him for forty years. He was very alert and active, still doing some paper work in his profession although he had been retired for a number of years. I tried to match him with a few ladies but either they disapproved of his smoking or he found them too staid and stiff. One day he called to say he was now in a relationship with a family friend and instructed me to thrown out his file. I never threw out files because I know the stability of most relationships. So I wished him good luck and put his file into the inactive.

A couple of times over the next few months, I called to see how things were going and to ask him if he wanted more introductions. He was still in the relationship but he appeared to be very unhappy. It seemed the woman in question was trying to make him over and disapproved of his smoking. He said, "For the right person, I would quit!"

To myself, I said quietly, "That's what they all say." Then I asked him to keep me posted as to his status and said good-bye. About a year later, I received a phone call from a woman who had read an article about me in a newspaper. She had been moved to call and inquire about the service. I chatted with her, trying to be realistic about the shortage of men in her age group. In spite of this she made an appointment to come in.

Joan was a petite, attractive English woman in her middle sixties. A widow and a survivor of a bad relationship, she seemed eager to meet a nice man. I took her on for a special rate because she seemed to be a "picky" one. Although very pleasant, I saw traces of anger in her lovely face and I felt that she could be quite critical.

When it came time to match her, Peter came into my mind as he was European and seemed to be from the same social class, with similar interests. However, I wasn't sure if he was available. I showed her some other profiles and told her I would get back to her.

The other gentlemen did not materialize, but when I called Peter, he was sufficiently disillusioned with his relationship that he agreed to meet Joan. She was a bit skeptical, because of his smoking and his age. However, they both agreed to meet.

A day or two later, when I arrived at the office, there was a message to call Peter. My first reaction was that she had changed her mind and was not going to meet him after all. I gritted my teeth and returned his call. To my surprise, he said in an elated voice. "I met Joan last night and I fell in love with her at first sight. Don't introduce her to any more men." I thought that's wonderful but what does she think?

I found out soon enough as she called to say she had met him and that he was coming on awfully strong. She found him blatantly honest about himself and his life and she wasn't sure how to take him. He wanted her to meet all his friends and to go on a cruise with him. I thought, that would keep her busy to awhile until I can find someone else for her.

About three weeks later, another message from Peter awaited me when I arrived at the office! My reaction was, oh no! She has broken up with him. Expecting to hear a tale of woe, I listened while he informed me he and Joan were engaged. He also said they were going on the cruise together and a trip to Europe to meet his family. Not believing what I heard, I called her. It was true! She had found him to be a sincere and loving man and she had agreed to marry him.

My reservations didn't end there. I kept thinking that once they were on a trip together, the trouble would begin and their wedding plans could still end up out the window. Since I had been invited to the wedding, I called one day to ask directions, fully expecting it to be called off. Instead, she told me they were more in love than ever, that the trips had strengthened their relationship.

They had a lovely wedding. He quit smoking and took up tennis to please her. He started going to her church after not attending since his first wedding. She left her job and started writing novels and typing reports for his work. On a regular basis they go to Hawaii, Europe and Nova Scotia where his son lives. They have a beautiful home, started a new set of china and have many wonderful friends. They claim after three or four years that their relationship gets better and better and that they have a fairy tale life. Whenever I see them they both look fantastic and all the anger is gone from her face.

I had another interesting surprise when a thirty-seven year old female physician, Roberta married an engineer. She had been one the clients that I had acquired from the previous owner. One day she called me in tears to tell of an abusive relationship that had just ended. Still very unhappy, she expressed a desire to meet someone else and wanted a family then she told me she wanted to meet someone younger than herself. I listened, but felt skeptical because the younger men who wanted children were looking for younger women than she. She asked to be put on hold for a while until she could heal for a while.

A couple of months later a young engineer, named Vlad, joined. He was tall, dark and handsome. He requested a woman young enough to have children, since he had never married. I began calling all the tall attractive young career women I had on file. It seemed that none of them were interested in meeting him at that time. I had eliminated Roberta because of her age. It was my husband who suggested her so I decided to reconsider her as a potential. When I examined her file, I saw that she was second generation European and fit his specifications in working part time and she was tall enough The only problem was her age. I presented her profile to him expecting him to refuse. However, he decided to meet her, to trust my judgment and to be open-minded about the whole thing. Since she was a doctor, he decided to ask her about the possibility of children. Unlike the lawyer, I spoke of in Chapter 16, he was willing to give it a chance.

After their first meeting, she called to thank me for the introduction to such a nice person. He called to say that she was intelligent, interesting, tall and wasn't a high-powered career woman. She appeared to be everything he had requested and that he would talk to her about them having children.

A few months later, I received an announcement that they had been married. She had found someone younger than herself (only two months younger.) He had found what he was looking for as well. I lost touch with them but hope they are the proud parents of some lovely children.

Clients who met dozens of people but nothing permanent ever happened were the ones who would sometimes surprise me the most. I had labelled many of them as hopeless. One of these was a thirty-year old woman, who I had decided was a confirmed spinster. She had a good job; a good sense of humour but was not very attractive or slim. She was quite concerned with a man's appearance and had met a lot of men but found something wrong with each.

She had been on file about eighteen months when a young realtor joined. He was a newcomer to the city and wanted to marry and have a family. Since he preferred a full-bodied woman, I thought of Lorraine, but had a number of others in mind as well. Much to my surprise, he met only Lorraine and they were engaged in a few months. I attended their wedding by the ocean and the last I heard, they were parents of a young son.

One client I had labelled as unmatchable was a man of about forty, who hiked a hundred hours a week. He spent every waking hour hiking. Thinking he would never have time for a relationship, I put his file on hold. About five years later I signed up a woman who wanted to spend her spare time hiking. They hit it off well, as well as I could determine.

I came to realize that some clients were choosers and others were the chosen. Humphery, the young scientist who married the second twin in Chapter 4 about the twins, was a chosen one.

Another surprise was a man in his forties, Harry who I had inherited from the previous owner and was a confirmed bachelor. I couldn't successfully match him because he was so independent. He was always going bear hunting and other such activities with his buddies. The women I introduced him to ended up aggravated with him because he didn't want to spend more time with them. One woman he liked was a realtor, Nora, who had an aggressive manner and a deep voice. She didn't like him because he was too old.

I finally introduced him to a costume designer, Marie, who said she didn't want to meet anyone who "took up all her time". She too had an aggressive manner, a deep voice and worked an 80-hour week. They hit it off because they were both so busy and could only spend some quality time together, once in a while. I was surprised that this match worked out.

In time I came to know that matching had very little to do with what I did or thought. It seemed that some matches were made in Heaven and that they only happened through me. I often felt that I was doing nothing other than providing the means for which two people destined to marry, could come together.

Chapter 19   The End

My goal, my whole life's purpose became that of holding the agency together, building it up so I could eventually sell it and get my money back. My goal also included making it into the best and most honest and successful service in Vancouver. So for five years, one and three quarters when I was with my husband and over three on my own, this became my only reason for living. I lived, breathed, ate and slept the business. I had no personal life except what my close friends and church activities could provide. I rarely took a weekend off and seldom left the city for any type of vacation. I always worked Saturdays and at the end of the day or week, I would treat myself to a dinner and a carafe of wine at a restaurant.

I attempted to numerous times over the five years to sell the business, listing it with realtors, business brokers and finally placing ads in the local and national newspapers on my own. Yes, there were people who were interested. I did receive one offer during the first year, which I kicked myself for not taking. At that time, I still felt I could retrieve all my investment. Several people phoned about it and a number came to see me and to look at it. But all of them, when they saw the small profits, realized they could not live on what I lived on. Some of them had no money of their own and were looking at borrowing from a bank and the prospects of making a living, paying off the loan scared them off. Even the dreamers became disillusioned with the prospect.

The truth was that I lived very frugally myself and had no

debts or liabilities. Occasionally I subsidized my income by doing some substitute teaching for the school board. In my absence, I would get the receptionist in my packaged office to take messages or hire someone to come in for a few hours. At least, it provided me with a slight break from the day-to-day anxiety of running the office.

Since the agency was my whole life, I lacked the support of other human beings. Since it occupied all my time, energy and thought, I was plagued by insomnia, anxiety attacks and bouts of severe depression. My bills for prescription drugs were high. I experienced one severe cold, lung and sinus infection after another. Doctors were fed up with seeing me in their offices.

I can't say it was all an experience from hell, but enough of it was so that it affected my life and health. There were some rewarding encounters and some people I enjoyed very much, who became friends. However the bad out weighed the good most of the time. I kept thinking that I had to begin having a life of my own again and I dreamed of being free from it all and walking away with my big cheque from it.

As I mentioned earlier, during the five years regardless of my goal setting, affirming success, praying, trying new advertising and promotion methods, the annual income remained about the same. In the final year, there was a change. The telepersonals came into being. Advertisers in any newspaper could meet a half dozen people for about thirty-five dollars and there were no interviews, forms to fill out or time to wait. It was quick, easy and cheap. My business and all the other agencies were feeling the brunt of it.

Over the years, I was determined. I vowed I would never put another dime into the business for any reason at all. I stuck to that vow to the very end. However, I had come to the place where technology had changed things. If I wanted to keep up with the times, I discovered I would have to invest another $10,000 to get an automated telephone system. When I examined my feelings, I realized there was nothing in me that could keep me going in this business for another day! I was totally burned out.

All my attempts at selling the business had failed. I started phoning friends, clients and anyone who had expressed any interest in the business. I came up with zip.

I decided to take a few days off and go to Vancouver Island to get clear in my mind what my next step would be. I wanted to be away from the noise and confusion of the city and to relax in a natural setting. I left my loyal assistant in charge of the office. While there I got clear that the step to take was to close the business. On my way to the ferry, I stopped to treat myself to a meal and a glass of wine. A romantic singer crooned some old songs. As I listened to the lovely strains of music, I realized how long it was since I had had a life. I was so busy creating lives for others that I had completely neglected my own.

It was time to end it. I couldn't afford to lose anything else of myself while hanging onto something that was doomed from day one. I had already lost a lot of my money, my Siamese cat, my peace of mind. I had also gone through menopause, my hair was almost completely gray and my youthful appearance had gone. I had no more time or anything else to lose.

Only the logistics of ending the business remained. It was already complete in my mind and heart. I had a few ideas on what my next move would be. I started to call other agencies; an act, which I had earlier decided, would be my last course of action. My very last resort was to close it, disconnect the phone and disappear. I really didn't want to do that unless I was desperate. Nor could I refund a lot of money.

An international conglomerate in the introduction business had moved into town, a few months earlier. I made my first phone call to them. A woman who was the sales manager agreed to come and see me that week at my office! I felt hopeful.

She arrived, big, fat and fifty, reminded me of my predecessor. Her proposal was that she would take over my clients if they each paid her company $300.00 I knew that I could not do that to my clients. I also learned that the huge video introduction service that had been my archrival since the beginning was also going out of business and she was taking over their clients for a charge of that amount. I refused her knowing there had to be a better way.

That left me with three other agencies. A young woman whom I had heard a lot of complaints from clients who had joined and claimed they had not met anyone ran one. I didn't think that agency would be the one. The second one had recently started up and was claiming to do intros by computer. I wondered if they would like some of my clients to help them get started. The young lady I called said she would discuss it with her partner. I never heard from her again. I was left with a service that had also been a rival. Taking the bull by the horns, I called and asked if I could come and see them. The wife asked what it was regarding so I told her at first I wanted to sell my files. They invited me to an interview the following week.

I went to their shabby office the next week, frightened out of my wits. Of course they weren't interested in buying my clients but were willing to take them over if I was going out of business. We both agreed to consider it for a few days and get back to each other. Since my back was against the wall, I had no choice but to say yes.

They asked for a list of clients and their ages, which they approved. They ones they didn't want, I kept. Thankfully most of those were expired memberships. Then we signed an agreement stating that they were taking over x number of files at no charge, for the purpose of matching. They took me to lunch a couple of times and spoke to them about selling for them on commission. Then they picked up the files accepting them all and left.

I contacted all my clients by phone telling them that another company was taking over their files and that I would still be involved. I gave them my new address and phone number. Even though my heart ached about the whole thing, the end of my dream, the end of my relationships with people I loved. I felt I had done the best I could. I felt I had ended the best way I could. I felt confident that this couple would do their best to match my clients and complete the contracts I had with them. I felt grief-stricken but relieved.

After they loaded the files into their car, they assured me they would call me about doing some selling for them. I was not really convinced but at that moment I had no other offers. I left the office that day for the last time, except for cleaning it.

I have heard that we die as we lived! If this is true for organizations, it was true for Renaissance. It began, lived and was destined to be in conflict. The next morning I was awakened by the telephone. It was the lady from the other agency telling me how none of my files were any good and that that they were giving them back to me. She called me a crook, a terrible businessperson, told me that they didn't want me to work for them. The worst of it all was that I would have to start all over again to find a place for the clients. I kept saying, "but you agreed to take them." She hung up in my ear.

Being entirely alone with this situation, I had to talk to someone. I phoned my estranged husband. He was sympathetic and asked me to give him a few moments to think about it. When he called back he calmly said, "A deal is a deal. They approved the customer list before taking it over. They signed a legal document agreeing to take them over. Then they accepted the files, signed, sealed and delivered. Don't accept the files back." I decided to stick to this. I decided not to accept any deliveries or phone calls from these people. They would have to live with the files and their obligation. I felt certain they had done what they did to get me out of business and never had any intention of honouring the agreement. I then took an unlisted telephone number and became a recluse.

The ending of the business was not at all like I had imagined it would be. There were no shaking hands with the new owner, no triumphant eyeing my big cheque. In fact, I felt sick, as sick as I had been the day I bought it, as sick as I felt the first few days in the office, as sick as I felt the day I fired my husband, as sick as I felt the day I left him.

But it was over at last. I could get on with the rest of my life, whatever that may mean. The end of an era had taken place. I was an empty shell. I would have to gather my strength to recover, to recuperate, to heal and to rise again to a new life. I could find out who I was without the agency, I could now plan a new life, to attempt to regain a life I had given up for a dream which proved to be a nightmare. I felt very strange but was determined to recover. I was free at last. I did recover some of my investment in the form of a tax refund.

Thank You

Thank you for buying and reading this book and for trusting me to entertain and inform you. I hope you'll consider writing a review about *The Pink Rose & Love Was My Business: Memoirs of a Matchmaker* online in the book listing's review section at any online retailer. It would be a huge honor if you did. And very much appreciated!

Best wishes always,

Sylvia

22409518R00124

Made in the USA
Columbia, SC
31 July 2018